THE DAVISON ORCHARDS COOKBOOK

THE Davison Orchards COOKBOOK

FAVOURITE RECIPES FROM
THE FARM AND FAMILY

Rachel Davison • Tamra Davison • Laura Shaw

TOUCHWOOD

This book is dedicated
to the next generation:
Tyson, Spencer, Caleb, Heidi, Anna, Levi,
Emily, Jacob, Jane, and John

May the LORD bless you
And keep you;
The LORD make his face shine upon you
And be gracious to you;
The LORD turn his face toward you
And give you peace.
—*Numbers 6:24–26*

The Generations That Shape Us

Left
Tom and May Davison

Below
Ted Davison with his children, Bob and Pat, shortly before he passed away

---

Each one of us has a story. We all come from somewhere and we are all shaped by our family history and the generations that came before us. As a family, we, the Davisons, feel blessed to be able to look back on our history with mostly pride and admiration. Here is a peek into our story.

Tom and May Davison—otherwise known as Uncle Tom and Auntie May—immigrated to Canada from England in 1927 and, in 1933, settled on the land we farm today. Although the new land presented fresh opportunities, Tom and May's days were spent doing what they had to do each day to make it to the next. With great tenacity and sheer hard work, they paved the way for what we enjoy today. Auntie May was not known for her cooking skills, but she will forever be remembered for her hospitality. Whenever a Davison child needed a quiet place to think or a safe space to let down their guard, they would head to the old farmhouse (now the Farmhouse Café) to see Auntie May. Out would come cookies and tea. The tea was always served in the child's very own fancy china teacup. It was a time for relaxation and conversation, a connecting point, bridging the gap between generations and ideas. Tom and May never had any children of their own, but when Tom's brother, who immigrated with him, died, the couple was good to his son and daughter, Bob and Pat Davison.

Above left
Bob Davison in the orchard

Above right
Dora Davison

Right
Tom and Tamra Davison

In his teenage years, Bob, known today as Grandpa Bob, spent a lot of time in the orchard helping his Uncle Tom. At the age of 17 he took over the farm when Uncle Tom passed away from cancer. He had to learn, often through trial and error, how to grow apples and run the business. At the age of 20 he married Dora, and together they raised six children—Joyce, Linda, Tom, Sharon, Erica, and Nate—and built a reputation of being true to their word, having a good work ethic, and extending hospitality to all. Dora, known by everyone as Nana, has the amazing gift of being able to use a little to produce a lot. She was known for being adept at both cooking and baking, and her kitchen seemed to produce an unending supply of apple slices to feed harvest crews, skilfully prepared soups to satisfy the hungry crowds at lunch time and hearty meat pies to end the day off right. Nana and Grandpa Bob have always had an open door policy, welcoming in anyone who knocks for a coffee break and a visit.

Their son Tom grew up watching his mom and dad work hard to put food on the table. Despite the back-breaking work for small returns, he too fell in love with the land and being a part of the miracle of producing quality food. After high school, he went to college in Alberta to study agriculture. There he met a young woman named Tamra, who was studying fashion design. The two were soon married. After being away from the farm for a few years, they wanted to go back and work the family land. At the time, the farm did not bring in enough income to support two families. Tom and Tamra therefore decided to use their education and skills to try their hand at direct-marketing their own produce, and so Davison Orchards Country Village was born in 1985. What

DAVISON
ORCHARDS
Vernon, B.C.
DAVISON ORCHARDS
VERNON, B.C.
DAVISON ORCHARDS
VERNON B.C.

Above
Lance Davison, Kevin Shaw, Grandpa Bob, and Tom Davison

started out as a "honk for service" apple stand has morphed into a thriving agri-tourism business complete with kids' play areas, a petting zoo, tractor tours, and a bakery and café where the farm-grown produce is sold as pies, soups, jams, and much more. As the farm grew, so did their family. Tom and Tamra were blessed with four children: Leah, Laura, Danica, and Lance. The kids grew up helping on the farm in different capacities and learned from a young age the value of hard work and hospitality. Tom and Tamra's hospitality did not stop with opening the doors of their farm, however. Tamra is an amazing cook and is always blessing others by inviting them into her home. Everyone is welcome: whether it's Walter Gretzky or the kids' friends from school.

Much like their dad, Laura and Lance grew up amid the hustle and bustle of the farm. Lance was drawn to growing fruits and vegetables from a young age, whereas Laura found herself gravitating toward the bakery, where the farm produce was turned into fresh pies, muffins, and other treats. In 2012, Lance, with his wife Rachel (me), and Laura, with her husband Kevin Shaw, officially committed to the family farm as a career. Our families have grown and we now have eight children between us, all running rampant on the farm. Laura and I both enjoy cooking with seasonal ingredients, taking advantage of what is ripe and turning it into hearty meals

and delectable desserts and preserving as much as possible to last throughout the winter months. This is our food philosophy, both at home and at the farm. This simple approach to eating is very much the same as that of the generations that came before us, and we are grateful to be able to pass these skills and ideas on to our children, as well as to you.

Writing this cookbook has been a very personal experience. Our family has been sharing our food and recipes with people in one way or another for over 90 years, but writing this book has felt like opening up our personal life for our visitors and social media followers to step into. Like the generations before us, we want to be hospitable, to invite people to sit at our tables for seasonal meals, cake and coffee, or tea served in china teacups. By compiling our favourite recipes and sharing our story with you in this book, we feel we are doing just that. And as you read through the pages, we hope that this book will draw family and friends around your table to celebrate the ones who came before you and bring you closer to the ones you share your life with right now. Each one of us has a story. No one's story is perfect and we cannot change what has gone on before us. But in order to move ahead, it is important to look back and be thankful for those who shaped us. Remember, we are all a part of the generations.

Top
Lance and Rachel Davison with their children

Bottom
Kevin and Laura Shaw with their children

Cook's Notes

The majority of the recipes in this book have either been handed down through our family from generation to generation or come from our family's farm, Davison Orchards in Vernon, British Columbia (look for recipes marked "A Farm Favourite"). The rest of the recipes either come courtesy of close family friends or have been developed by us in recent years. Each one has been tested rigorously and adapted where necessary for today's home cook. We emphasize using fresh, local ingredients as much as possible. Our desire throughout the writing process was to stay true to our roots and to throw open our kitchens for you to step inside and cook alongside us. We would be honoured if this book becomes batter-splashed and dog-eared with use as our favourites become your favourites. Here are some brief tips and explanations to increase your chances of success as you dive into these recipes.

General Best Practices

- Carefully read each recipe through before you begin to cook or bake to ensure that you have the proper ingredients and adequate time.
- Do your prep—for example, peeling, chopping, or pitting—before you begin to cook or bake to simplify the task.
- Wash the dishes as you go to keep a large pile from accumulating.
- For your convenience, we have included both hands-on time and total time required for each recipe. We timed the recipes from start to finish, so they include time for the prep work. Please remember, though, that the timings are only guidelines. For example, give yourself extra time if you are making a recipe for the first time.

Terminology

When it comes to preparing ingredients, there are many different terms that can get confusing. Here is a breakdown to help you out:

- Minced refers to cutting something as small as possible.
- Diced means to cut into small, evenly sized pieces, approximately ⅛ inch square.
- Chopped means to roughly cut into approximately ¼-inch pieces.
- Cubed refers to cutting something into evenly sized, bite-size pieces.

You'll notice slightly different wording across the recipes, because we all have our own preferences. Unless otherwise specified, you can use either a bowl and a wooden spoon (Rachel's preferred method) or an electric hand-held or stand mixer (Laura's and Tamra's preferred method). Use whatever method you are comfortable with, but take note of the terminology in the recipes:

- Whisking means to mix vigorously with a wire whisk or whisk attachment to add air to the batter or, in the case of whisking dry ingredients, to smooth out lumps.
- Beating refers to using a wooden spoon or a paddle attachment at high speed to cream the ingredients.
- Stirring means to mix at a medium-low speed until the ingredients are fully combined (this can be done with any utensil or attachment).
- Folding means to gently fold the batter over itself until just combined. This is best done by hand with a wooden spoon or spatula.

Baking with Butter versus Margarine

We are going to go out on a limb here and admit something that is not going to be very popular. Ready? The Davison girls bake with margarine. I know. Now you are judging us, but don't close the book! Please hear me out first.

I (Laura) like butter. I like it on my toast, my pancakes, and my corn on the cob. Rachel likes butter. Tamra likes butter. Nana LOVES butter. She is even known to liberally butter crackers before she adds a piece of cheese. We are all pro-butter. We will not argue with you that, on its own, butter tastes 100% better than margarine.

But we don't bake with it. I mean, traditionally. Yes, there are certain recipes that must be made with butter instead of margarine, but as a general rule it's not what we use in our baking. This is consistent across the generations of Davisons and across all our households.

My in-laws scratch their heads at me, unable to reconcile how I could commit such a culinary atrocity (using margarine, that is) while being a committed home baker. The tension came to a head a few years ago, and so we decided to end the argument once and for all by having a bake-off and blind-tasting Classic Chocolate Chip Cookies (page 207) made with margarine versus butter. Here's the hard truth—and I have to admit that I, too, was shocked by the results—we couldn't taste the difference!

So now you know. I trust our reputation precedes us and you don't throw us out as frauds. The thing is, this book is made up of authentic family recipes, and either we were going to adjust all these recipes to fit with current mainstream ideas, or we were going to provide you with the real deal. So here is the real deal. We are staying true to our roots.

Unless only butter is specified, margarine and butter can be used interchangeably in these recipes. If you choose to use margarine, use a high-quality baking margarine (the kind that comes in ½-cup squares, not the spreadable kind that comes in a tub). In the recipes that specify butter, we recommend using salted butter. Please feel free to use whatever suits your preference. I won't judge you, and maybe you won't judge me.

Canning Tips

A handful of the recipes in the Preserves chapter (pages 224–255) need to be processed by canning, which is the art of preserving produce at its peak freshness in an airtight jar. This can feel like a daunting undertaking, so if it's an option, try to find a mentor with canning knowledge from your area who can work alongside you or be available to answer your questions. If you aren't able to find a mentor, you can find lots of information in books and online. Do some research, but don't let yourself become overwhelmed. Remember that the basics are very simple. One crucial thing to remember, though, is that canning guidelines vary from region to region because of elevation and humidity levels, so be sure to use specific guidelines for your area. Here are some general tips to bear in mind when you're canning:

- Inspect your jars for nicks and cracks, especially around the rim. They need to be in great condition. Use new sealers every year. Rings can be reused if they are free from rust.
- Always sterilize your jars and lids before using. To sterilize the jars, preheat the oven to 225°F. While it heats, wash the jars in warm soapy water. Rinse them thoroughly and place them in the oven for 10 minutes. To sterilize the lids, place them in a small pot and cover them with water. Bring the water to a boil over high heat and then immediately turn the temperature to low to keep the water hot until you are ready to use the lids. Do not allow your lids to boil for a prolonged time. This will weaken the rubber on them.
- Use good quality fruits and vegetables. Inspect them carefully and set aside any that are spoiled. Wash your produce in cool water before preserving it.
- Some useful equipment includes a large pot, a rack or liner to go under the jars in the pot (it is essential to have space between the bottom of the jars and the pot to keep the jars off the heat source and allow the boiling water to surround the entire jar), a jar lifter to remove the jars from the hot water, and a magnet lifter to lift the lids out of the boiling water. A funnel for filling jars is also handy.
- The water in your pot should cover the jars by about 1 inch. After you place the jars in the pot, wait until the water has come back to a boil before you start your timer.
- Allow the finished product to sit undisturbed on the counter for 24 hours before storing. This will allow time for the jars to fully seal. Check the seal by gently pressing on the centre of the lid. If it is solid, it is sealed, but if it pops up and down, it is unsealed. Place any unsealed jars in the refrigerator and use them within one month.
- Store sealed jars in a cool, dark, dry area. Most preserves have a shelf life of one year. High-sugar products, such as canned fruit, are safe to keep for up to two years. Keep opened jars in the refrigerator and use them within one month.
- Give yourself enough time so that you can be relaxed and enjoy the process.

Produce

How to buy: Eating produce straight from your own garden is the best way to ensure that your produce is fresh. However, you and I both know that this is not always possible or feasible. And that is totally ok. Thankfully there are many hard-working farmers out there who are passionate about growing amazing fruits and vegetables. Our husbands are some of those farmers, and we can personally attest that they work tirelessly to supply our customers with superior quality produce with incomparable flavour. When you're shopping for produce, the best thing you can do is have an idea of where it came from. If you have the chance to talk to the farmers, don't be afraid to ask questions about the produce; they are usually happy to share their knowledge. If you are shopping in a large grocery store, look for locally grown options when available. Check for freshness by looking for things like green, pliable stems, firmness, and fragrance (if the cantaloupe doesn't stink, it won't taste great!). Don't beat yourself up, though, if you buy produce from outside your local area. Let's be thankful that we have access to such a variety of produce year-round, regardless of where it was grown!

Organic versus conventional: Although many of our methods at Davison Orchards would be considered organic-approved, we never claim to be organic. We feel that the organic label has somewhat lost its meaning and has become more about marketing than environmental stewardship. We are absolutely committed to farming in the most sustainable way possible. We use many "green" methods, including drip irrigation, mulching, and crop rotation. You can be confident that when you eat something grown or made at Davison Orchards, you are making a choice to eat food that has been farmed in a way that protects our land and community for future generations. When you're shopping in a large grocery store, try to remember that the "organic" label does not mean the product is healthier. Instead of focusing on the labels, seek to work a variety of fruits and vegetables into your diet.

Using local year-round: As previously mentioned, we believe the best way to eat in a sustainable and healthful way is to eat locally grown food. So what do we do in the dead of winter? During the summer, when fresh produce is in abundance, we delight in tucking away some to use throughout the lean months. This can be as simple as boiling a little more corn than we need for supper and slipping the extra into the freezer, or as hard-core as having a full-blown canning bee! For tips on how to store, freeze, and can produce, see pages 10–14, and for ideas on what to preserve, see chapter 8 (pages 224–255).

Standard Ingredients

We are farmers and can't help but be practical! We believe in using what is on hand instead of making a special trip to the store or going outside our budget for a specific ingredient. Here is a guideline for following our recipes. Unless otherwise specified:

Fruit

- Apples and pears are whatever fresh apples or pears you have on hand or have access to. Most of our recipes have a list of suggestions.
- Frozen fruits and vegetables can be used from frozen and baking/cooking times remain the same.
- Raisins can be any type and don't need to be soaked. Our favourite is Thompson seedless raisins.

Dairy

- Butter is salted.
- Margarine is baking margarine.
- Cheddar can be mild, medium, or old.
- Milk is any fat level of cow's milk. The recipes have not been tested for non-dairy milks.

Spices, herbs, and broth

- Paprika is any type. Use your favourite.
- Parsley is fresh and can be flat-leaf or curly (your choice).
- Salt is table or sea salt (your choice).
- Pepper is freshly ground black.
- Broth is homemade or store-bought. While homemade is always best, store-bought broth can be used in any of our soups. Simply reduce the added salt if you are using store-bought.

Extracts and juices

- Lemon juice can be freshly squeezed or bottled.
- Vanilla extract can be pure or artificial (your choice).
- Store-bought, clarified apple juice cannot be substituted for Davison Apple Juice. If you are able to source another local apple cider or juice that is not heat-treated, feel free to use that instead.

Guide to Preserving Fruits and Vegetables

Most fruits and vegetables only have a short season in which they are locally available. During the summer months there is always something fresh to enjoy, but the winters can feel long! When produce is stored properly, however, it is possible to eat local year-round. In this section, we share some tips on how to store, freeze, and can some of our favourite fruits and vegetables.

For detailed instructions on how to can, see the canning guidelines on page 8 and the Canned Peaches recipe on page 233.

When you're freezing produce, always use bags or containers that are designed specifically for the freezer. They have thicker walls, which will protect the contents from freezer burn.

Dehydrating is another great way to store produce. Almost anything can be dried! My favourites are pears, apples, cherries, prune plums, and hot peppers. You can use a dehydrator (simply follow the manufacturer's directions) or your oven (use the method on page 221). The timings will vary depending on the produce, the thickness of the slices, and the humidity of the day.

Vegetables

Corn

- **Storing:** Corn is best eaten the same day it is picked, as the natural sugars begin converting to starch the moment it leaves the stalk. Keep cobs in the refrigerator in a plastic bag until you're ready to use them, up to 2 days.

- **Freezing:** Plunge the husked corn cobs into boiling, salted water. Bring the water back to a rolling boil, then turn off the heat and cover the pot. Let the corn sit in the hot water for 5 minutes before placing it in ice water for 2 minutes. Cut the kernels off the cobs. A Bundt pan is a brilliant tool for this job. Hold the cob in the centre and cut off the kennels, letting them fall into the pan. Transfer the kernels to freezer bags and lay flat to freeze. Freeze for up to 8 months. Heat through to eat as a side or use in any recipe that calls for frozen or canned corn.
- **Canning:** Not suitable for home canning.

Green Beans

- **Storing:** Refrigerate beans in a plastic bag in the vegetable drawer for up to 4 days.
- **Freezing:** Trim the stems. Cut the beans to your desired size (I like 1-inch pieces or whole). Blanch the beans by plunging them into boiling, salted water. Bring the water back to a boil for 2 minutes, then transfer the beans to ice water for 2 minutes. Drain off any excess moisture, pat dry, and freeze on a baking sheet until solid. Transfer to a freezer bag and freeze for up to 8 months. Eat as a side dish by cooking the beans on the stovetop in boiling water for 3–5 minutes, or use in any recipe that calls for green beans.
- **Canning:** Not suitable for home canning.

Sweet and Hot Peppers

- **Storing:** Refrigerate whole peppers in a plastic bag in the vegetable drawer for up to 2 weeks. Wrap half-used peppers in a paper towel and keep in the vegetable drawer for up to 3 days.
- **Freezing:** Wash and pat dry, then seed and cut the peppers to your desired size. Freeze them on a baking sheet until they are solid. Transfer to a freezer bag and freeze for up to 4 months. Use frozen peppers in chilies, soups, and casseroles.
- **Canning:** Not suitable for home canning.

Squash and Pumpkins

- **Storing:** For long-term storage, wash in a 4:1 solution of water to vinegar or a sink full of water with 1 Tbsp of bleach. Submerge the squash or dip a towel in the solution and wipe each squash off. Let the squash dry completely before storing in a cool, dry, dark place. Typically, squash stores well for up to 5 months.
- **Freezing:** Preheat the oven to 375°F. Cut the squash in half and remove the fibrous strands and seeds. Place it face side down on a parchment-lined baking sheet and bake until the flesh is soft and pierces easily with a fork, about 45 minutes. Cool, peel, and purée in a blender or food processor. Pack in freezer bags and freeze for up to 1 year. Thaw to use in your favourite baked goods or soups.
- **Canning:** Not suitable for home canning.

Tomatoes

- **Storing:** Tomatoes should never be stored in the refrigerator. Instead, spread them out in a single layer on the counter or in an open box and store them at room temperature. Keep them away from other fruits and vegetables, as they produce a gas that causes ripening.
- **Freezing:** Wash and pat the tomatoes dry. Cut out the core, then place them in a freezer bag and freeze for up to 5 months. The skins will slip off easily once they are partially thawed. These are perfect to use in any soups, stews, or sauces.
- **Canning**: Blanch the tomatoes by plunging them into boiling water for 30 seconds, then transfer to ice water for 1 minute. Slip off the skins, and core. Pack tightly into sterilized quart jars (see page 8) so that no air remains. Add ¾ tsp salt and 2 Tbsp bottled lemon juice (do not use freshly squeezed, as you cannot control the pH level) per jar.

Can in a hot-water bath for 35 minutes, or according to your area's canning guidelines.

Zucchini

- **Storing:** Refrigerate in a plastic bag in the vegetable drawer for up to 1 week.
- **Freezing:** Do not peel the zucchini, as most of the nutrients are found in the skin. Wash and cut them into your desired size. Plunge the chopped zucchini into boiling, salted water. Bring the water back to a boil, boil for 2 minutes, and then transfer the zucchini to ice water for 2 minutes. Drain off any excess moisture and freeze in freezer bags for up to 8 months. Use in casseroles and soups. Alternatively, wash and grate the raw zucchini. Pack into freezer bags in amounts that suit your recipes. To use, half-thaw and drain off any excess moisture. Use half-frozen to ensure that some of the moisture is going into your food. Grated zucchini is perfect for using in baking and sauces.
- **Canning:** Not suitable for home canning.

Fruits

Apples

- **Storing:** Store in a cool, dry place, such as a basement, a cold room, or the garage in the winter. Certain varieties store better than others. Some excellent keepers are Honeycrisp, Granny Smith, Ambrosia, Gala, and Mutsu. Sort apples in long storage now and again to remove any damaged fruit. Remember, one bad apple spoils the bunch!
- **Freezing:** Peel, core, and slice the apples. Toss 4 cups of prepared apples with ½ cup of granulated sugar to prevent browning. Place in freezer bags and freeze for up to 8 months. To use, half-thaw and drain off excess moisture. Use in baked goods or to make a quick pot of applesauce.
- **Canning:** My favourite way to preserve apples in jars is to make applesauce (page 255). Pour the prepared applesauce into sterilized pint jars (see page 8), leaving ½ inch of headspace. Place in a hot-water bath for 13 minutes, or according to the canning guidelines of your area.

Apricots

- **Storing:** Store apricots at room temperature, in a single layer, to ripen. They are ripe when they are slightly soft, but be careful how often you squeeze to check because you'll bruise them every time!
- **Freezing:** Rinse (no need to dry), slice in half, and remove the pits. Place in freezer bags and freeze for up to 1 year. Use them from frozen in baked goods.
- **Canning:** See page 231.

Blueberries and Raspberries

- **Storing:** Keep the berries dry and store in shallow, loosely covered containers in the refrigerator. Only wash immediately before using.
- **Freezing:** Rinse and place on a towel to dry slightly. Place the berries in a single layer on a baking sheet and freeze until solid. Transfer to freezer bags and freeze for up to 1 year. Thaw the berries to use as a topping for pancakes, yogurt, or ice cream, or use frozen in baked goods, milkshakes (page 265), or smoothies.
- **Canning:** Fill sterilized pint jars (see page 8) with clean berries. Boil together a syrup of 3:1 water to sugar. Pour the syrup over the berries to fill the jars, leaving ½ inch of headspace. Wipe the rims clean and close with a new lid. Place in a hot-water bath for 12 minutes, or according to the canning guidelines for your area.

Cherries

- **Storing:** Store cherries in the refrigerator in a loosely closed plastic bag for up to 4 days.
- **Freezing:** Rinse (no need to dry), pit, and

stem the cherries. If desired, slice them in half. Place the prepared cherries in a single layer on a baking sheet and freeze until solid. Transfer to freezer bags and freeze for up to 1 year. Use frozen in baking and smoothies. Thaw to eat on pancakes or in yogurt.
- **Canning:** Rinse (no need to dry), pit, and stem the cherries. Follow the canning instructions for blueberries.

Peaches

- **Storing:** Always handle peaches with care, as they bruise easily. Spread them out in a single layer to ripen at room temperature. A peach is ripe when it smells fragrant and the hollow around the stem is golden.
- **Freezing:** Blanch by placing the ripe peaches in boiling water for 30 seconds. Transfer to ice water for 1 minute. Slide off the peels and slice or chop the fruit. Stir together 1 Tbsp granulated sugar and 1 Tbsp of a preservative such as Fruit Fresh. Sprinkle the sugar mixture over 4 cups of prepared peaches and toss to coat. Transfer to a freezer bag and freeze for up to 6 months. Use from frozen in baked goods or smoothies, or thaw the peaches to use as a topping for yogurt or pancakes.
- **Canning:** See page 233.

Pears

- **Storing:** Pears should be stored in a cool, dry place such as a basement, a cold room, or the garage in the winter. D'Anjou pears are incredible keepers and can last up to 4 or 5 months! Move to room temperature to ripen. Bartlett pears are ripe when they turn a mellow yellow colour. D'Anjou and Bosc pears barely change colour when ripe, so check for ripeness by gently pressing near the stem. When it's slightly soft, it's ripe.
- **Freezing:** Not suitable for freezing.
- **Canning:** Peel, core, and slice the pears and place in sterilized jars (see page 8. Make a syrup by boiling a 3:1 solution of water to sugar. Pour this over the pears to fill the jars, leaving ½ inch of headspace. Place in a hot-water bath for 15 minutes for quart jars and 13 minutes for pint jars, or according to the canning guidelines for your area.

Prune Plums

- **Storing:** Store at room temperature out of direct sunlight for up to 7 days. Prune plums keep fairly well if they aren't too warm.
- **Freezing:** Rinse (no need to dry), slice in half, and remove the pits from the plums. Place in freezer bags and freeze for up to 1 year. Use from frozen in baked goods such as crisps or Nana's Plum Cake (page 185).
- **Canning:** Rinse (no need to dry), slice in half, and remove the pits. Pack the plums into sterilized pint jars (see page 8). Make a syrup by boiling a 3:1 solution of water to sugar. Pour over the plums to fill the jars, leaving ½ inch of headspace at the top. Place in a hot-water bath for 13 minutes, or according to the canning guidelines for your area.

Strawberries

- **Storing:** Keep the berries dry and store in loosely covered shallow containers in the refrigerator, preferably the fruit drawer, for up to 3 days. Only wash immediately before using.
- **Freezing:** Rinse and place on a towel to dry slightly. Remove the tops, slice if desired, and freeze on a baking sheet until solid. Transfer the berries to freezer bags and freeze for up to 1 year. Thaw the berries to use as a topping for pancakes, yogurt, or ice cream, or use frozen in baked goods, milkshakes (page 265), or smoothies.
- **Canning:** We don't recommend canning strawberries as they get a little mushy, but if you would like to give it a try, follow the canning directions for blueberries.

5

Chapter 1

Quick Breads

Our Daily Bread

Every home cook should have a full repertoire of quick bread recipes that they are comfortable whipping up. This chapter will help you achieve that. It is chock full of reliable muffin, scone, loaf, and biscuit recipes. These are our personal favourites—quite literally our daily bread.

In her younger years, Nana Davison was the master of quick breads. Everyone who entered her house was immediately sat down at the kitchen table, given a cup of coffee or tea, and offered a slice of whatever loaf she had on hand, slathered with copious amounts of butter. She has been making Cheese Biscuits (page 31) since she was about 10 years old, so for the last 80-plus years! In her younger days, she could whip up Raisin Scones (page 33) in no time flat. Nothing beats those scones fresh from the oven, spread with butter and Apricot Jam (page 251). The thought alone weakens our knees and makes our mouths water!

These days it is not very popular to eat carbs for breakfast, lunch, and supper as well as snacks. But honestly, that is the way we all grew up! There was no money for convenience snacks from the grocery store. In the winter months we didn't have fresh produce on hand, so we ate muffins at coffee break and biscuits with our supper. We were healthy and happy and never thought anything of it. We now feed our families in a very similar way. Don't misunderstand us: we eat copious amounts of fruits and vegetables! But we are not scared of polishing off a loaf at 10:00 AM. We work hard, we stay active, and we eat carbs—a lifestyle we highly recommend.

The Davison Girls: Rachel, Tamra, and Laura

Toasty Pear Muffins

12 large muffins
15 minutes prep
35 minutes total

These muffins hit the spot on a foggy morning alongside a steaming cup of Earl Grey tea—Auntie May's favourite brew. The teacup in the photo is a family treasure, as it comes from Auntie May's collection. Back when she lived in what is now the Farmhouse Café, Auntie May had a specially designated teacup for each of the Davison children to use when they popped in for a visit. **Rachel**

- ⅔ cup chopped pecans, divided
- 1½ cups all-purpose flour
- ¾ cup wheat germ
- ½ cup brown sugar, lightly packed
- 1 tsp baking powder
- 1 tsp baking soda
- ½ tsp salt
- ½ tsp ground cardamom (see note)
- 2 eggs
- ¾ cup plain yogurt
- ⅓ cup canola oil
- 1 tsp vanilla extract
- 2 very ripe pears, peeled, cored, and mashed with a fork

Note: If you're not a fan of cardamom, or you don't have any on hand, swap it out for the same volume of ground cinnamon.

Preheat the oven to 375°F. Line 12 muffin cups with muffin papers or coat with cooking spray.

Spread ½ cup of the chopped pecans out on a rimmed baking sheet. Bake until toasted and fragrant, 3–4 minutes. Remove from the pan and set aside to cool. Do not turn off the oven.

In a large bowl, stir together the flour, wheat germ, sugar, baking powder, baking soda, salt, and cardamom.

In a separate bowl, whisk together the eggs, yogurt, oil, and vanilla. Stir in the mashed pear.

Pour the wet ingredients over the dry ingredients and stir gently until just combined. Fold in the toasted pecans.

Divide the batter evenly among the prepared muffin cups. Sprinkle the remaining pecans on top. Bake until the top of a muffin springs back when gently pressed, 15–17 minutes. Allow to cool in the pan for 3 minutes before transferring to a wire rack to cool completely.

Store in an airtight container on the counter for up to 2 days or in the freezer for up to 3 months.

Chocolate Zucchini Muffins

24 muffins
15 minutes prep
35 minutes total

Let's be honest, these are more cupcakes than muffins. But they are packed with vegetables, dairy, and grains, which sounds like a wholesome breakfast or snack to me! All joking aside, these delicious muffins can easily be converted to a cake. Simply stir the batter more vigorously and pour it into a greased 9 × 13-inch cake pan. Top as directed and bake at 325°F for 45 minutes. **Tamra**

- ½ cup butter or margarine, softened
- ½ cup canola oil
- 1½ cups granulated sugar
- 2 eggs
- ½ cup sour cream
- 1 tsp vanilla extract
- 2½ cups all-purpose flour
- ¼ cup cocoa powder
- 1 tsp baking soda
- ½ tsp ground cinnamon
- ½ tsp salt
- 2 cups grated and lightly packed zucchini
- ½ cup semisweet chocolate chips
- ½ cup unsweetened shredded coconut

Preheat the oven to 350°F. Line 24 muffin cups with muffin papers or coat with cooking spray.

Cream the butter and oil with the sugar until light and fluffy. Add the eggs one at a time, beating well after each addition. Stir in the sour cream and vanilla.

In a separate bowl, whisk together the flour, cocoa, baking soda, cinnamon, and salt. Add to the creamed mixture, stirring until just combined.

Fold in the grated zucchini.

Divide the batter evenly among the prepared muffin cups. Sprinkle the top of each one with the chocolate chips and coconut.

Bake until a toothpick inserted in the centre comes out clean, about 20 minutes. Let the muffins cool in the pan for 4 minutes before removing to a wire rack to cool completely.

Store in an airtight container on the counter for up to 2 days or in the freezer for up to 3 months.

Pumpkin Chocolate Chip Muffins

16 muffins
15 minutes prep
35 minutes total

Without a doubt, these are my family's favourite muffins. Something about the ooey-gooey chocolate paired with hearty pumpkin and a hint of cinnamon keeps us all coming back for more. In the late autumn I like to cook an oven-full of pumpkin and bake dozens of these to have on hand in the freezer. If you don't have applesauce, simply increase the oil to ¾ cup. **Rachel**

---

2 eggs
¾ cup granulated sugar
1 cup pumpkin purée (see note)
½ cup canola oil
¼ cup applesauce, homemade (page 255) or store-bought
1½ cups all-purpose flour
1 tsp baking soda
1 tsp baking powder
½ tsp ground cinnamon
½ tsp salt
1 cup semisweet chocolate chips

Note: Most store-bought cans of pumpkin purée are 28 oz/796 mL, so you won't use a full can for this recipe. However, there are other great pumpkin recipes in this book (pages 29, 183, 205) to help you use it all up! You can also freeze the extra purée in portion sizes for the recipes of your choice or store it in an airtight container in the refrigerator for up to 3 days.

Preheat the oven to 375°F. Line 16 muffin cups with paper liners or coat with cooking spray. Pour a little water into the cups you aren't using so that they don't burn. Set aside.

In a medium bowl, whisk together the eggs and sugar until well combined. Add the pumpkin purée, oil, and applesauce and whisk vigorously to combine.

In a separate bowl, stir together the flour, baking soda, baking powder, cinnamon, and salt. Add to the pumpkin mixture and stir with a wooden spoon until just combined. Fold in the chocolate chips.

Spoon the batter into the prepared muffin cups, filling them ¾ full. Bake until the top of a muffin springs back when gently pressed, 16–20 minutes. Allow to cool in the pan for 3 minutes before removing to a wire rack to cool completely.

Store in an airtight container on the counter for up to 2 days or in the freezer for up to 4 months.

Pumpkin Biscuits

10–12 biscuits
15 minutes prep
30 minutes total

A few years ago, Nana was in the hospital for an extended period. During that time, Grandpa Bob would join us for supper most nights, which was a treat for us all. One evening, I served these biscuits alongside supper. Grandpa must have eaten five of them! On the way out the door he slapped my husband on the shoulder and shouted, "Your wife sure can make biscuits!" We all had a good laugh, and this recipe has been a regular at our table ever since. **Rachel**

- 1¾ cups all-purpose flour, plus more for dusting the counter
- 1 Tbsp brown sugar
- 2½ tsp baking powder
- ½ tsp salt
- ¼ tsp baking soda
- ½ cup cold butter or margarine, cubed
- ¾ cup pumpkin purée (see note on page 27)
- ⅓ cup milk

Preheat the oven to 425°F. Line a rimmed baking sheet with parchment paper.

In a large bowl, whisk together the flour, sugar, baking powder, salt, and baking soda. Using a pastry blender, a fork, or your hands, cut in the butter until the mixture resembles coarse crumbs. The butter pieces should be no larger than a pea. Alternatively, pulse the dry ingredients and the butter in a food processor fitted with the steel blade.

In a glass measuring cup, stir together the pumpkin and milk. Pour over the dry mixture and stir with a wooden spoon to make a soft dough.

Turn the dough out onto a lightly floured surface and knead gently 6–8 times, just enough to bring it together into a ball (see note on page 31). Pat the dough with your hands, or roll lightly with a rolling pin, to about ½ inch thick. Cut into 3-inch squares. Place the biscuits on the prepared baking pan, close together for soft-sided biscuits or 1 inch apart for crusty ones.

Bake until lightly browned on top, 13–15 minutes. Serve hot with a slather of butter.

These are best eaten right away, but leftovers can be stored in an airtight container on the counter for up to 2 days or frozen for up to 2 months.

Nana's Cheese Biscuits

15 biscuits
10 minutes prep
25 minutes total

Every home cook needs a quick, foolproof biscuit recipe that bakes up so light and fluffy that they look like a genius made them. Here is the one that Nana has been making for the past 80 years! These biscuits are simple and fast, and are the perfect accompaniment to any soup, stew or casserole. For a classic tea biscuit, simply omit the cheese. **Rachel**

- 2½ cups all-purpose flour, plus more for dusting the counter
- 3¾ tsp baking powder
- ¾ tsp salt
- ½ cup cold butter or margarine, cubed
- ¾ cup shredded old cheddar cheese
- 1¼ cups milk

Note: When you're working with quick doughs, a little bit of kneading improves the quality of the final product but use a gentle touch. Too much handling makes for tough biscuits!

Preheat the oven to 450°F. Line a rimmed baking sheet with parchment paper.

In a large bowl, whisk together the flour, baking powder, and salt. Using a pastry blender, a fork, or your hands, cut in the butter until the mixture resembles coarse crumbs. The butter pieces should be no larger than a pea. Stir in the cheese. Pour the milk over the dry mixture and stir to make a soft dough.

Turn the dough out onto a lightly floured surface and knead gently 8–10 times, just enough to bring it together into a ball. (See note.) Pat the dough with your hands, or roll with a rolling pin, to about ¾ inch thick. Using a 2½-inch circular cookie cutter, cut out your biscuits, rerolling once if necessary. Place the biscuits on the prepared baking pan, close together for soft-sided biscuits or 1 inch apart for crusty ones.

Bake until lightly browned on top, 10–13 minutes. Serve hot alongside a bowl of soup, or spread with butter and honey.

These are best eaten right away, but leftovers can be stored in an airtight container on the counter for up to 2 days or frozen for up to 2 months.

Nana's Raisin Scones

8 scones
10 minutes prep
25 minutes total

For a time, Nana made these scones daily in the Davison Farmhouse Bakery. However, they are best served hot and do not have a good shelf life, so we eventually removed them from our repertoire. They have been sorely missed, particularly by my husband, Tom, and so we're sharing the recipe so you can serve them, piping hot, slathered with butter and jam, from your own kitchen. **Tamra**

- 2½ cups all-purpose flour, plus more for dusting the counter
- ¼ cup granulated sugar
- 3¾ tsp baking powder
- ¾ tsp salt
- ½ cup cold butter or margarine, cubed
- 1 cup raisins
- 1¼ cups milk
- ¾ tsp vanilla extract

Preheat the oven to 450°F. Line a rimmed baking sheet with parchment paper.

In a large bowl, whisk together the flour, sugar, baking powder, and salt. Using a pastry blender, a fork, or your hands, cut in the butter until the mixture resembles coarse crumbs. The butter pieces should be no larger than a pea. Alternatively, pulse the dry ingredients and the butter in a food processor fitted with the steel blade. Stir in the raisins. Mix together the milk and vanilla. Pour the milk mixture over the dry mixture and stir to make a soft dough.

Turn the dough out onto a lightly floured surface and knead gently 8–10 times, just enough to bring it together into a ball (see note on page 31). Pat the dough into a circle about ¾ inch thick and 10 inches in diameter. Cut it into 8 wedges. Place the wedges on the prepared baking pan, keeping them close together but with just enough space between each one to make room for rising.

Bake until lightly browned on top, about 13 minutes. Serve warm, with a slather of butter and a generous amount of your favourite jam.

These are best eaten right away, but leftovers can be stored in an airtight container on the counter for up to 2 days. They do not freeze very well.

Chocolate Cherry Scones

12 scones
15 minutes prep
40 minutes total

These scones are the reason I freeze sweet cherries when they're in season. They are absolutely decadent—perfect for an outdoor tea party in June, or for indulging in while you curl up with a good book on a dreary day in February. If you don't have cherries on hand, blueberries are (almost) equally delicious, especially if you top the scones with Lemon Drizzle Icing (page 59). **Rachel**

- 2½ cups all-purpose flour
- ½ cup granulated sugar
- 2 tsp baking powder
- ½ tsp salt
- ½ cup cold butter or margarine, cubed
- ¾ cup milk
- 1 egg
- ½ tsp vanilla extract
- 1 cup halved and pitted fresh or frozen sweet cherries
- ¾ cup chopped chocolate; chocolate chip size is perfect (I use dark)
- Coarse sugar for sprinkling (optional)

Preheat the oven to 400°F. Line a rimmed baking sheet with parchment paper.

In a large bowl, stir together the flour, sugar, baking powder, and salt. Using a pastry blender, a fork, or your hands, cut in the butter until the mixture resembles coarse crumbs. The butter pieces should be no larger than a pea. Alternatively, pulse the dry ingredients and the butter in a food processor fitted with the steel blade.

In a glass measuring cup, mix the milk, egg, and vanilla together. Pour this over the flour mixture. Stir gently with a wooden spoon until the flour is almost moist. Add the cherries and chocolate. Stir until just combined. The dough will be wet and sticky. If you overmix this dough, it will turn pink from the cherries and your scones will be tough.

Spoon the dough onto the prepared baking sheet, making 12 evenly sized scones. If desired, sprinkle coarse sugar on top of each scone. Bake until golden brown and firm to the touch, 20–25 minutes.

These scones are delicious warm or cold. Leftovers can be stored in an airtight container in the freezer for up to 3 months.

Peach Apricot Loaf

2 loaves
20 minutes prep
1 hour, 15 minutes total

When the last of the apricots give way to the first of the peaches, it is time to make this delectable loaf. These two soft fruits pair well together, but because of the timings of their seasons, they don't often get to share the limelight. Fresh and frozen fruit both work well in this recipe, and if apricots are not available, you can substitute the same volume of dried apricots (no need to soak them before using). **Laura**

- 1¾ cups granulated sugar
- 1 cup canola oil
- 4 eggs
- 1 Tbsp vanilla extract
- 3 cups all-purpose flour
- 2 tsp baking powder
- 1½ tsp baking soda
- 1 tsp salt
- 2 peaches, peeled, pitted, and chopped (about 2 cups)
- ¾ cup pitted and chopped apricots
- ½ batch Davison's Snow White Topping (page 39)

Preheat the oven to 350°F. Coat two 5 × 9-inch loaf pans with cooking spray, or grease with butter or margarine.

In a large bowl, whisk together the sugar and oil until creamy. Add the eggs one at a time, beating well after each addition. Stir in the vanilla.

In a separate bowl, whisk together the flour, baking powder, baking soda, and salt.

Add the dry ingredients and the fruit alternately to the egg mixture, starting and ending with the dry ingredients. Mix with a wooden spoon until just combined.

Divide the batter evenly between the prepared loaf pans. Sprinkle the tops with the crumble topping.

Bake on the centre rack until a toothpick inserted in the centre comes out clean, 50–60 minutes. Let the loaves sit in the pans for 15 minutes before removing to a wire rack to cool completely.

Store in an airtight container on the counter for up to 2 days, or wrapped in plastic wrap in the freezer for up to 3 months.

Davison's Snow White Topping

3 cups
10 minutes prep
10 minutes total

This is a beautifully simple, white crumb topping, perfect for giving muffins and loaves that finishing touch.

---

1 cup all-purpose flour
1 cup granulated sugar
½ cup cold butter, cubed

In a medium mixing bowl, combine the flour and sugar.

Using a pastry blender, a fork, or your hands, cut in the butter until the mixture resembles coarse crumbs. The butter pieces should be no larger than a pea. Alternatively, pulse the dry ingredients and the butter in a food processor fitted with the steel blade.

Use right away, or store in an airtight container in the refrigerator for up to 7 days or in the freezer for up to 3 months. You can use it from frozen.

Davison Farmhouse Zucchini Loaf

2 loaves
20 minutes prep
1 hour, 15 minutes total

If there's one thing we Canadians have in abundance at the height of the summer, it's zucchini. I like to grate large amounts to freeze in 3-cup portions (see page 13). When you're using zucchini from the freezer, add it to the recipe when it's still half-frozen. That way you don't lose all the moisture when it thaws. If it's totally thawed, drain about half the water from the bag before you add it to your dough. **Laura**

- 1 cup canola oil
- 1 cup granulated sugar
- ⅓ cup brown sugar, lightly packed
- 3 eggs
- 2 tsp vanilla extract
- 3 cups all-purpose flour
- 1 tsp baking soda
- 1 tsp baking powder
- 1 tsp salt
- 1½ tsp ground cinnamon
- 3 cups grated and lightly packed zucchini
- 1 cup semisweet chocolate chips
- ½ cup chopped walnuts (optional)
- ½ batch Davison's Snow White Topping (page 39) (optional)

Preheat the oven to 350°F. Coat two 5 × 9-inch loaf pans with cooking spray, or grease with butter or margarine.

Beat the oil with both sugars until creamy. Add the eggs one at a time, beating well after each addition. Stir in the vanilla.

In a separate bowl, whisk together the flour, baking soda, baking powder, salt, and cinnamon.

Add the dry ingredients and grated zucchini alternately to the sugar mixture, starting and ending with the dry ingredients. Stir until just combined. Do not overmix. Fold in the chocolate chips and walnuts (if using).

Divide the batter evenly between the 2 prepared loaf pans. Sprinkle the loaves with the topping (if using).

Bake on the centre rack of the oven until a toothpick inserted in the middle of a loaf comes out clean, 50–60 minutes. Allow the loaves to cool for 15 minutes in the pan before turning out onto a wire rack to cool completely.

Store in an airtight container on the counter for up to 4 days, or place in a freezer bag and freeze for up to 3 months.

A FARM FAVOURITE

Chai-Spiced Pear Loaf

2 loaves
30 minutes prep
1 hour, 40 minutes total

Look no further for a solution to what to do with the rapidly ripening pears accumulating on your kitchen counter. The browned butter frosting paired with the chai spice makes this loaf both unique and extraordinary! Eat it for breakfast, serve it for coffee break, or enjoy a slice after dinner for dessert. **Rachel**

Chai-Spiced Pear Loaf

- 2 cups all-purpose flour
- 1 cup whole wheat flour
- 3 tsp baking powder
- 1½ tsp salt
- 1 tsp ground cinnamon
- ⅔ tsp ground cardamom
- ½ tsp ground ginger
- ⅓ tsp ground black pepper
- ¼ tsp ground allspice
- ¼ tsp ground cloves
- ¼ tsp ground nutmeg
- 1¾ cups granulated sugar
- 4 eggs
- ¾ cup milk
- ¾ cup canola oil
- 3 medium pears, peeled, cored, and chopped

Browned Butter Frosting

- ¼ cup salted butter
- 2 cups icing sugar
- 4–5 tsp boiling water
- 1 tsp vanilla extract

A FARM FAVOURITE

For the loaf

Preheat the oven to 350°F. Coat two 5 × 9-inch loaf pans with cooking spray, or grease with butter or margarine.

In a large mixing bowl, whisk together both flours, the baking powder, salt, and spices.

In a smaller bowl, whisk together the sugar, eggs, milk, and oil. Pour this wet mixture over the flour mixture and stir until just combined. Add the chopped pears and fold to incorporate.

Divide the batter evenly between the prepared loaf pans. Bake until firm to the touch and a toothpick inserted in the centre of a loaf comes out clean, 60–70 minutes. Allow the loaves to cool in the pan for 15 minutes before turning out onto a wire rack to cool completely.

For the frosting

In a small saucepan, melt the butter over medium heat. Heat, swirling, until golden brown and nutty, 5–7 minutes.

Pour the browned butter into a bowl. Whisk in 1 cup of the icing sugar. Add 3 tsp of the boiling water and the vanilla, whisking until smooth.

Whisk in the remaining icing sugar until the mixture is thick but pourable. Add more water, 1 tsp at a time, as necessary.

Drizzle the cooled loaves with a generous amount of browned butter frosting.

Store leftovers in an airtight container on the counter for up to 2 days. Unfrosted loaves can be placed in a freezer bag and frozen for up to 3 months. Let frozen loaves thaw completely at room temperature before drizzling with frosting.

Chapter 2

Breakfast and Brunch

Simple Traditions

One of my very favourite family traditions is Sunday morning pancakes. This tradition started in the Davison household when my husband was a young boy. Tom rarely does the cooking, except for on Sunday mornings when the huge stainless steel bowl, eggs, flour, and oil make an appearance in his kitchen. He doesn't exactly use a recipe (making the documenting of his pancake recipe a tall order), but every time he puts a little of this and a scoop of that into the bowl, out come the fluffiest, most golden-brown pancakes you've ever seen!

As teenagers, the Davison children brought all sorts of friends home for Dad's pancakes. Bear in mind that when I say Sunday morning breakfast, I'm not talking about a leisurely 10:00 AM brunch. This is a 7:00 AM, get-up-and-at-it tradition. So you can picture the scene: Dad, who's been up for hours, whistling and flipping pancakes while blurry-eyed, bed-headed teens are finding spots around the table, sneaking pieces of bacon and plucking blueberries out of the bowl.

Fast forward 15 years and we find Lance wielding the flipper and the table crowded with our five young children who inhale pancakes like a garburator. There is endless chatter, spilled milk, requests for peaches, crumbs flying, singing, and sticky fingers; it is a (may I never forget) beautiful chaos! We've kept the tradition alive, and our hope is that one day we will be blessed with a tableful of teenagers, disarmed by pancakes.

In order to truly experience the Sunday morning pancake ritual, you need to know how to top your pancakes. Butter and syrup just doesn't cut it at our house. Upon receiving a pancake, our children immediately pile it high with yogurt, "apricot stuff" (our name for canned apricots that have been puréed into a syrup—see page 231), fruit such as strawberries, blueberries, and peaches, and a drizzle of maple syrup. Once they have applied every topping on the table it can safely be dubbed a Papa Pancake, as this is how Tom is known to enjoy his.

Simple traditions like this help keep us grounded. This breakfast is something to look forward to throughout the week, without adding stress to our already busy lives. We hope that, like us, our children will look back on this with fondness and perhaps even carry on the tradition themselves.

Rachel

MAPLE SYRUP
SIROP D'ERABLE

Sunday Morning Pancakes

15 large pancakes
10 minutes prep
25 minutes total, plus resting

If there is one thing my dad is known for, it's his Sunday morning pancakes. For decades this breakfast has been a tradition in the Davison household. It started when we were very young, and continued when we were teenagers and young adults. Our friends were always welcome, and it was not unusual for us to have more than 20 people around the table for breakfast before church. The tradition is still alive and, as my kids like to say, "There's nothing as good as Papa's Pancakes!" **Laura**

2¼ cups all-purpose flour
¾ cup whole wheat flour
¼ cup granulated sugar
2 Tbsp baking powder
¾ tsp salt
2 eggs
2¼ cups milk
⅓ cup canola oil
½ tsp vanilla extract
Butter, for frying

In a large bowl, whisk together both flours, the sugar, baking powder, and salt. Crack the eggs into a separate bowl and beat lightly. Add the milk to the eggs and whisk until combined.

Pour the wet ingredients over the dry and stir with a wooden spoon until combined. Some lumps are ok. Fold in the oil and vanilla. If you have time, it's best to let the batter sit for 15 minutes before cooking.

Melt about 1½ tsp of butter on a griddle heated to about 325°F (alternatively, use a skillet over medium heat on the stovetop). Drop the batter by large spoonfuls onto the hot griddle. When bubbles form throughout the pancake, flip it and fry until cooked through, about 4 minutes. You do not need to rebutter the griddle each time.

Serve immediately with your favourite toppings (see page 48 for Davison Family favourites).

Store the leftover batter in an airtight container in the refrigerator for up to 2 days or cook all the pancakes and keep them in the refrigerator for up to 3 days. Reheat leftovers in the toaster for a quick breakfast.

Rachel's Granola

8 cups
15 minutes prep
40 minutes total

This has been my favourite granola my entire life. I make it in double batches and freeze it in repurposed glass jars. That way, when somebody is unwell or just needs a pick-me-up, I have a sweet, homemade gift all ready to give away. This recipe is very easy to customize. Feel free to exchange the nuts for any kind you like, swap the pepitas for sunflower seeds, or mix and match with different combinations. If you're looking for a gluten-free granola, omit the wheat germ and make sure your oats are certified GF. As long as you keep the dry to wet ratio the same, you can basically do whatever you like! **Rachel**

- 2 cups quick oats
- 2 cups large-flake oats
- ¾ cup chopped almonds
- ½ cup chopped unsalted peanuts
- ½ cup pepitas (shelled pumpkin seeds)
- ½ cup unsweetened shredded coconut
- ½ cup wheat germ
- ¼ cup freshly ground flaxseed
- ¾ cup honey
- ½ cup canola oil
- 2 tsp ground cinnamon
- ½ cup dried fruit such as Craisins, dried cherries, apple chips, etc. (optional)

Preheat the oven to 325°F. Line a rimmed baking sheet with parchment paper.

In a large bowl, mix together the oats, almonds, peanuts, pepitas, coconut, wheat germ, and flaxseed.

In a small saucepan, mix together the honey, oil, and cinnamon. Bring to a boil over medium-high heat, stirring regularly. Carefully pour over the dry ingredients. Stir with a wooden spoon until evenly coated.

Spread the granola evenly onto the prepared baking sheet. Bake for 15 minutes. Remove from the oven and sprinkle the dried fruit overtop (if using). Stir the granola and return to the oven until nicely toasted, about 10 minutes. If you have chosen not to add dried fruit, it is still important to stir the granola partway through baking to ensure even cooking.

Let the granola cool completely on the pan. Break it into chunks and serve over fruit and yogurt, on your breakfast cereal, or plain by the handful!

Store in an airtight container in the pantry for up to 3 weeks or in the freezer for up to 6 months.

Davison's Apple Cinnamon Buns

12 buns
35 minutes prep
3 hours total

For years I dreamed of learning how to make cinnamon buns. They were not something that I grew up watching my mom bake, so for a long time I saw them as being out of my league. I still remember the day in the Davison Farmhouse Bakery when one of the more experienced bakers taught me how to make this recipe. I tried to hide it, but I was absolutely ecstatic to be deemed worthy of learning the art of apple cinnamon buns. I can still remember her speaking to me in her strong European accent: "Tighten your tummy muscles, Laura. Use your whole body and rrrrroooll the dough! No! Don't strrrrretch it, Laura, rrrrroooll the dough!" **Laura**

Dough
- 1¼ cups warm water (approx. 110°F)
- ¼ cup granulated sugar
- 2½ tsp instant yeast
- 1 egg
- ¼ cup canola or vegetable oil
- 1 tsp salt
- 3–4 cups all-purpose flour

Sticky Bottom
- ¾ cup brown sugar, lightly packed
- ⅓ cup butter or margarine
- 3 Tbsp corn syrup
- 1½ tsp vanilla extract
- ¼ tsp salt
- 2¼ Tbsp hot water

Filling
- ½ cup brown sugar, packed
- 1 Tbsp ground cinnamon
- 4 Tbsp butter or margarine
- 1 medium apple

Vanilla Drizzle
- 1 batch Vanilla Drizzle Icing (page 59)

A FARM FAVOURITE

For the dough
In the bowl of a stand mixer fitted with a dough hook, combine the warm water, sugar, and yeast. Stir with a wooden spoon until incorporated and let sit for 5 minutes. Place the egg and oil in a glass measuring cup and beat lightly with a fork. Add to the yeast mixture along with the salt. Stir to combine.

With the mixer running on low, slowly add the flour, periodically scraping the bottom and sides of the bowl, until it has formed into a soft dough. Continue mixing, adding flour about 1 Tbsp at a time as necessary, until the dough starts to come off the sides of the bowl and bounces back when you press it with your index finger, about 7 minutes. Shape the dough into a ball and place it in a large greased bowl. Cover with plastic wrap and let sit in a draft-free spot until doubled in size, about 1 hour.

For the sticky bottom
Meanwhile, in the bowl of a stand mixer fitted with a paddle attachment, beat the sugar and butter on high speed until light and fluffy. Add the corn syrup, vanilla, and salt. Mix until combined. Turn the mixer to low speed and slowly add the hot water. Turn the mixer to high speed and beat until fluffy and thick. Liberally spread the bottom and sides of a 9 × 13-inch baking dish with half of the sticky bottom mixture. Set the rest aside.

For the filling
About 10 minutes before you are ready to roll out your buns, mix together the sugar and cinnamon in a small bowl. Place the butter in the microwave and heat it on high power until it has almost melted. Peel and grate the apple. »

To make the buns

When the dough has doubled in size, dump it out onto a lightly floured work surface. Roll into a rectangle about 12 × 18 inches. Be gracious with yourself. It doesn't need to be perfect!

Spread the softened butter all over the dough, right to the edges. Next, sprinkle on the cinnamon-sugar filling mixture, leaving a bare ½-inch strip along the top of the long end of your rectangle to help with sealing the buns. Squeeze the excess juice out of the grated apple and sprinkle the apple evenly over the cinnamon sugar.

Gently roll the dough away from you to create a log, sealing it at the part covered in only butter. Place it seam side down on your work surface. Using a serrated knife, cut the dough into 12 evenly sized buns. Place all 12 rolls, evenly spaced, in your prepared pan. Cover with plastic wrap and let the buns rise until they are puffy and fill the baking pan, 45–60 minutes.

Preheat the oven to 350°F.

Remove the plastic wrap and bake the buns for 25 minutes. Remove from the oven and drop 1 tsp of the reserved sticky-bottom mixture on each bun. Spread evenly over the top and return the buns to the oven until the buns are golden brown and the middle bun bounces back when you press on it gently, 10–15 minutes.

Let the buns sit for 10 minutes while you prepare the icing (see page 59).

Drizzle the icing over the warm cinnamon buns.

These are best served warm, but leftovers can be stored in an airtight container at room temperature for up to 2 days.

Vanilla Drizzle Icing

½ cup
2 minutes prep
2 minutes total

Nothing finishes off a sweet treat like a drizzle of icing. It takes so little time to make and is as easy as 1-2-3. Vanilla is a classic flavour that goes well with almost everything. Lemon drizzle tastes like spring and pairs well with recipes starring berries. Maple drizzle transports you to autumn and is wonderful on scones or other baked goods.

---

1 cup icing sugar
1 Tbsp half-and-half cream
1 tsp vanilla extract (see note)

Note: This icing can be used to top lots of baked goodies in this book. You can also adapt the flavouring if you like.

Lemon Drizzle Icing: *Replace the cream with the same volume of freshly squeezed lemon juice and omit the vanilla.*

Maple Drizzle Icing: *Replace the vanilla with the same volume of maple extract.*

Using a teaspoon, stir the icing sugar, cream, and vanilla extract together in a small glass measuring cup. Add more cream if the icing is too thick or more icing sugar if it is too thin.

Drizzle over your dessert or quick bread.

Leftovers can be stored in an airtight container for up to 1 week in your refrigerator. You can warm up your icing for 10–20 seconds in the microwave to soften right before you're ready to use.

Zucchini Pancakes

12 pancakes
20 minutes prep
40 minutes total

During the winter months my family regularly enjoys potato pancakes. That's why this summer, when I was drowning in a mountain of zucchini, I decided to create another version of this family favourite: zucchini pancakes! It turned out to be a very versatile recipe. The pancakes make a great side dish for any supper or a satisfying light lunch served with tzatziki sauce. But they shine at the breakfast table when served with a fried egg and a link of sausage. **Rachel**

- 4 cups grated and lightly packed zucchini
- 1 clove garlic, minced
- ½ cup diced yellow onion
- ¼ cup grated parmesan cheese
- 1 tsp chopped fresh oregano
- 1 tsp chopped fresh chives or green onions, plus more for garnish
- ¾ tsp salt
- ½ tsp pepper
- 2 eggs, lightly beaten
- 1 cup all-purpose flour
- 2 tsp baking powder
- Olive or canola oil, for frying
- Sour cream, plain yogurt, or tzatziki sauce, for serving

Place the grated zucchini in a large bowl. If there is excess moisture, pat the zucchini with a paper towel to pull some out. Add the garlic, onions, parmesan, and seasonings. Stir to combine.

Add the eggs and stir until evenly distributed. Fold in the flour and baking powder until incorporated.

Warm 1 Tbsp of oil in a large skillet over medium heat. Drop the batter by rounded spoonfuls into the hot pan, flattening it with the back of the spoon to resemble the shape of a pancake. Cook until golden brown and cooked through, about 3 minutes per side. Repeat with the remaining batter, adding more oil as necessary in between batches.

Serve them as you cook them with a dollop of sour cream, plain yogurt, or tzatziki sauce and garnish with snipped chives.

Leftovers can be stored in an airtight container in the refrigerator for up to 2 days. Reheat in the frying pan.

Crêpes

10–12 crêpes
5 minutes prep
25 minutes total

My oldest brother isn't much of a cook (he even hired me to make his lunches during his bachelor years), but he sure can churn out the crêpes! You knew it was going to be a great day when you woke up to Andrew in the kitchen, flipper in hand and music blaring, tossing these crêpes onto every plate that made its way to the stove. **Rachel**

- 3 eggs
- 1¾ cups milk
- 1½ cups all-purpose flour
- ½ tsp salt
- Butter, for frying
- Your favourite toppings

Preheat the oven to 175°F.

Place the eggs, milk, flour, and salt in a blender in that order. Blend until smooth.

Lightly coat the bottom of a nonstick skillet with butter and warm it over medium heat. You only need to butter it to cook the first crêpe. Once it's hot enough for a drop of water to sizzle in the pan, pour about ¼ cup of batter into the centre of the pan and swirl it around to make a thin layer that covers the bottom of the pan. Cook until the edges start to curl, about 1 minute. Flip and cook the other side until done, about 30 seconds.

Place the cooked crêpes on a plate, cover loosely with aluminum foil or a lid, and keep them warm in the oven while you cook the rest.

Serve with fresh strawberries and Nutella, peaches and whipped cream, or sweet cherries and maple syrup (or whatever you like).

Cover leftovers with plastic wrap and store in the refrigerator for up to 3 days. Reheat in the microwave one at a time for about 30 seconds.

Zucchini and Herb Mini Quiches

12 mini quiches
20 minutes prep
45 minutes total

Resembling a popover when pulled from the oven, these fun mini quiches are amazing served hot and fresh. Sometimes, however, I make a batch to keep in the refrigerator or freezer. That way I can pull one out in the morning, heat it through, and enjoy it sandwiched in a toasted English muffin. **Tamra**

- 1 Tbsp olive oil
- 1 cup grated and lightly packed zucchini
- 1½ Tbsp chopped fresh chives
- 2 tsp chopped fresh parsley, divided
- 1 tsp chopped fresh thyme
- 8 eggs
- 1 cup shredded old cheddar cheese, plus more for topping
- ½ cup cottage cheese
- ½ tsp salt
- ¼ tsp pepper

Preheat the oven to 350°F. Line 12 muffin cups with muffin liners or liberally grease with butter or margarine.

Place the oil in a skillet and sauté the zucchini over medium heat until translucent and reduced but not browned, about 5 minutes. Remove from the heat and stir in the chives, 1 tsp of the parsley and the thyme.

Divide the mixture evenly among the 12 muffin cups.

Pulse the eggs, both cheeses, salt, and pepper in a blender or a food processor fitted with the steel blade for a few seconds, until well mixed but not puréed. Pour the egg mixture over the zucchini, dividing it equally among the muffin cups. Sprinkle a small amount of shredded cheddar cheese and the remaining parsley on top of each mini quiche.

Bake until set and firm to the touch, 20–25 minutes. Serve warm.

Leftovers can be stored in an airtight container in the refrigerator for up to 3 days or frozen for 4 months. Thaw and warm before eating.

Bacon and Asparagus Quiche

Serves 6
20 minutes prep
1 hour, 5 minutes total

The first shoots of asparagus that I find poking up out of the warming soil each spring feel like a gift from above. After a long winter, there is nothing like the enjoyment of fresh food, making this quiche the quintessential springtime brunch. **Tamra**

- 1 single-crust 9-inch pie shell (page 171)
- 8 stalks asparagus
- 6 eggs
- ¾ cup 3.25% milk
- 1¼ cups shredded Italiano cheese blend (provolone, mozzarella, Romano, Emmenthal)
- ½ tsp pepper
- ½ tsp garlic salt
- 4 slices bacon, fully cooked and roughly chopped

Line a 9-inch pie dish with the pastry.

Preheat the oven to 350°F. Put a medium pot of water on to boil.

Cut the heads off the top of the asparagus and set aside to use as a garnish. Thinly slice the asparagus stalks lengthwise. Place the slices in the boiling water. Bring the water back to a boil and simmer over medium heat for about 30 seconds. Remove the asparagus and rinse immediately with cold running water. Place it on a clean kitchen towel to dry.

In a medium bowl, whisk together the eggs and milk. Stir in the cheese, pepper, and garlic salt.

Cover the bottom of the pie shell with half the asparagus. Top with ¾ of the bacon, then the remaining asparagus. Pour the egg and cheese mixture over the asparagus. Garnish with the remaining bacon and asparagus heads, creating a pattern of your choice.

Bake until set and firm to the touch in the centre, about 45 minutes. Let stand for 10 minutes before serving. Serve warm or room temperature.

Leftovers can be stored in an airtight container in the refrigerator for up to 2 days. Reheat before serving.

Blueberries 'n' Honey Baked Oatmeal

Serves 6
15 minutes prep
1 hour, 10 minutes total
plus overnight chilling

I'm not much of a morning person, so the thought of creating a filling, healthy breakfast for my family every day is a bit overwhelming! This baked oatmeal solves that problem. Not only do you make it the day before so all you have to do is pop it in the oven in the morning, but it also reheats beautifully, allowing you to have it on hand throughout the week. Try it with diced apples (peeled or unpeeled) instead of blueberries for an autumn twist. **Rachel**

---

3 cups large-flake oats
2 tsp baking powder
1 tsp ground cinnamon
½ tsp salt
3 eggs
½ cup butter, melted
½ cup liquid honey
1½ cups milk
1½ cups fresh or frozen blueberries (or any other fruit or berry)
Cream, fresh fruit, and maple syrup, for serving (optional)

Coat an 8 × 8-inch glass baking dish with cooking spray, or grease with butter or margarine.

In a small bowl, stir together the oats, baking powder, cinnamon, and salt.

In a large bowl, whisk together the eggs, butter, and honey until well combined. Stir in the milk.

Fold the dry ingredients into the egg mixture. Stir in the blueberries. Pour the batter into the prepared dish.

Cover the dish with aluminum foil and place it in the refrigerator overnight. In the morning, place the dish into the cold oven. Turn the oven to 375°F and bake the oatmeal, covered, for 40 minutes. Remove the foil and bake until set in the centre, about 10–15 more minutes.

Serve warm with cream, fresh fruit, and maple syrup, if desired.

Leftovers can be stored in an airtight container in the refrigerator for up to 4 days. Simply reheat and serve for a quick weekday breakfast.

Chapter 3

Soups

The Soup Queen

When it comes to food, you can never go wrong with soup. A well-crafted pot makes for a soul-satisfying, nutritious, and economical meal both at noon and at the end of the day. I am sometimes referred to as the Soup Queen by my family. Now, I'm not convinced about the royal designation, but I do have a deep and sincere love for making soups. I get a real feeling of gratification from the knowledge that we are all getting a healthy dose of vegetables, broth, and much, much more every time the ladle dips into the pot. Making soup from scratch is really very simple, and no store-bought version will ever come close to matching the flavour and nutritional value.

For thirty years, I made large batches of everything to keep up with feeding my four children, my hungry farmer husband, and whoever happened to join us at the table. Soup was my best friend, as making a huge pot was quick and easy. My goal was to have enough leftovers to carry us through lunch the next day, although I rarely achieved that goal. But suddenly, in the blink of an eye, the kids grew up and moved out! Now it's just Tom and me at the table most nights. Old habits die hard, however, and I still find myself making huge batches of soup.

For those of you who find yourselves in a similar situation, just freeze some for when life is busy and you need an easy meal. I like to gift a jar of soup to a friend who needs encouragement or share some of my homemade goodness for lunch with Nana and Grandpa Bob. After all, soup is my love language!

More often than not, I don't follow the exact recipe I'm using. Rather, I improvise by adding a little more of this or that, or replacing one vegetable or spice with another. This can give an old recipe a fresh new twist, although there are times when sticking to the recipe may have been a better idea! But that's the beauty of soup. Unlike baking, it's not an exact science, so it suits my personality perfectly.

In this chapter you'll find many of our family favourites. If you are new to soup making, try each one by carefully following the recipe. Then, as your confidence and skills grow, you can start taking liberties to make adjustments tailored to your tastes. And who knows? Before long, you may just be known as the Soup Queen or King.

Tamra

A Gift for You!

Squash Soup Three Ways

Squash soup is a staple in every Davison home. There was a time when we were teased for our love of squash. When friends came over they were very suspicious of the smooth, orange concoction that Mom placed in front of them. But after the first sip, they were hooked! In recent years, squash has made a comeback, and it's no wonder. It is cheap, versatile, and delicious—not to mention a nutritional powerhouse. The following recipes are our favourites. We suggest trying all three to see which one you like the best.

Personalize your own bowl by garnishing your soup with fresh parmesan cheese, a splash of cream, crunchy croutons, pepitas (shelled pumpkin seeds), or freshly ground black pepper.

Each of these soups can easily be made gluten-free, dairy-free, and vegan by switching the chicken broth to vegetable broth or water and choosing appropriate garnishes. Enjoy!

Tamra's Squash Soup

Serves 6
15 minutes prep
45 minutes total

This is our family's favourite squash soup. I like to prep it in the morning before I head to work. I sauté the onions and carrots and then toss everything into the crock pot (see note). That way, lunch is ready when I am! This soup freezes beautifully, making it practical to produce in large batches. **Tamra**

- 1 Tbsp butter
- 1 medium yellow onion, roughly chopped
- 3 large carrots, cut into ½-inch pieces
- 1 large butternut squash, peeled, deseeded, and cut into 1-inch cubes
- 3–4 cups chicken broth
- ½–1 tsp salt
- ¼ tsp pepper
- 2 tsp chopped fresh thyme, or 1 tsp dried thyme
- Fresh parmesan cheese, croutons, half-and-half cream, pepitas, or pepper, for garnish (optional)

Note: To make this in a crock pot, follow the first step and then add everything to your crock pot. Cook on high heat for 4 hours or low heat for 8 hours. Blend to your preferred texture according to the method above.

In a large pot, melt the butter over medium heat. Add the onions and carrots and sauté, stirring occasionally, until the onion is translucent, about 5 minutes. Add the squash to the pot and sauté for 2 more minutes to deepen the flavour of the squash.

Pour the broth slowly into the pot, stopping just before it covers the vegetables (they should stick out of the liquid a little). Add the salt and pepper, as well as the thyme if you are using dried. Stir to combine. Cover and bring to a boil over high heat. Once the soup is boiling, turn the heat to low and simmer gently, stirring occasionally, until the vegetables are tender, 25–30 minutes. If you're using fresh thyme, add it in the last 5 minutes of cooking.

Remove the pot from the heat. Using an immersion or stand blender, carefully blend the soup until it is puréed and smooth. Remember, hot soup can easily scald!

Serve, garnishing as desired.

Leftovers can be kept in an airtight container in the refrigerator for up to 4 days or in the freezer for up to 4 months.

Silky Squash Soup

Serves 8
20 minutes prep
45 minutes total

This squash soup has a bit more dimension and a silkier texture (hence the name) than Tamra's. The ginger adds a nice touch, elevating the flavour profile, while the potatoes are the secret to the oh-so-soft consistency. This is a nice soup to serve to company for lunch or to give to a friend in need of a home-cooked meal. **Laura**

- 1 Tbsp canola or olive oil
- 1 medium yellow onion, roughly chopped
- 2 large carrots, cut into ½-inch pieces
- 3–4 cloves garlic, crushed and minced
- 1 Tbsp minced fresh ginger, or 1 tsp dry ground ginger
- 3 cups peeled, cubed yellow potatoes
- 1 large butternut squash, peeled, deseeded, and cut into 1-inch cubes
- 1 tsp salt
- ½ tsp pepper
- 4 cups chicken broth
- Fresh parmesan cheese, croutons, half-and-half cream, pepitas, or pepper, for garnish (optional)

Heat the oil over medium heat in a large pot. Add the onions. Sauté until the onion is translucent, about 5 minutes. Add the carrots and the garlic. If you are using fresh ginger, add that now as well. Sauté until the garlic is fragrant, 1–2 minutes.

Add the potatoes and squash. Season with salt, pepper, and the dry ground ginger, if you're not using fresh.

Pour the broth slowly into the pot, stopping just before it covers the vegetables (they should stick out of the liquid a little). Cover and bring to a boil over high heat. Once the soup is boiling, turn the heat to low and simmer gently, stirring occasionally, until the vegetables are tender, 20–25 minutes.

Remove the pot from the heat. Using an immersion or stand blender, carefully blend the soup until it is puréed and smooth. Remember, hot soup can easily scald!

Serve, garnishing as desired.

Leftovers can be kept in an airtight container in the refrigerator for up to 4 days or in the freezer for up to 4 months.

DAVISON

Autumn Harvest Soup

Serves 6
20 minutes prep
45 minutes total

Packed with fruits and vegetables, this soup makes me think of an autumn harvest. Thick, smooth, and slightly sweet, it is sure to please. The sweet potato adds a satisfying dimension, while the bay leaf keeps it grounded and decidedly savoury. **Rachel**

- 1 Tbsp butter
- 1 medium yellow onion, roughly chopped
- 2 cloves garlic, smashed and minced
- 2 large carrots, cut into ½-inch pieces
- 1 small butternut squash, peeled, deseeded, and cut into 1-inch cubes
- 1 small sweet potato, peeled and cut into 1-inch cubes
- 1 apple, peeled, cored, and chopped
- 1 bay leaf
- 4 cups chicken broth
- ½–1 tsp salt
- ½ tsp pepper
- Fresh parmesan cheese, croutons, half-and-half cream, pepitas, or pepper, for garnish (optional)

Melt the butter in a large pot over medium heat. Add the onion and sauté until translucent, about 5 minutes. Add the garlic and cook until fragrant, about 1 minute. Add the carrots, squash, sweet potatoes, apples, and bay leaf.

Slowly pour the broth over the vegetables, stopping when the broth almost covers the vegetables in the pot (they should stick out of the liquid a little). Season with salt and pepper.

Cover the pot and increase the temperature to medium-high. Bring to a boil. When the soup is boiling, turn down the temperature to low and gently simmer, stirring occasionally, until the vegetables are tender, 20–25 minutes.

Remove the pot from the heat. Discard the bay leaf. Using an immersion or stand blender, carefully blend the soup until it is puréed and smooth. Remember, hot soup can easily scald!

Serve, garnishing as desired.

Leftovers can be kept in an airtight container in the refrigerator for up to 4 days or in the freezer for up to 4 months.

Hamburger Soup

Serves 6
25 minutes prep
1 hour, 10 minutes total

Hamburger soup was my all-time favourite as a child, and with eight hungry mouths to feed, I'm certain it was a favourite of my mom's as well. This soup is hearty, healthy, and simple. The vegetables required can all be grown in a Canadian garden, and the end result equals more than the sum of its parts. How else but with soup can you feed your entire family with two potatoes and three carrots! **Rachel**

- ½ lb lean ground beef
- 1 medium yellow onion, diced
- 2 cloves garlic, crushed and minced
- 1 can (28 oz/796 mL) diced tomatoes and their juice, or 3 fresh tomatoes, peeled and diced
- 6 cups beef broth or 6 cups water + 1 Tbsp beef bouillon
- 2 cups washed and cubed potatoes
- 2 cups sliced carrots
- ½ cup chopped celery, including leaves
- Salt and pepper
- ¼ cup barley, rinsed and drained
- ½ cup fresh or frozen peas
- ¾ cup dry baby shells pasta (optional)
- ¼ cup chopped fresh parsley

In a large stock pot over medium heat, brown the beef and onions until the beef is no longer pink. Add the garlic and cook until fragrant, about 1 minute. Pour in the tomatoes and their juice and bring to a gentle boil over medium heat. Add the beef broth or water + bouillon. Bring back to a boil and add the potatoes, carrots, and celery. Season with salt and pepper to taste. Bring back to a boil and then add the barley.

Cover and gently simmer the soup over medium-low heat, stirring occasionally, until the vegetables and barley are almost tender, about 35 minutes.

Add the peas, pasta (if using), and parsley. Stir and cook until tender, about 10 minutes.

This soup is great served immediately, but it tastes even better the next day. We enjoy this soup with Pumpkin Biscuits (page 29) or Nana's Cheese Biscuits (page 31).

Leftovers can be stored in an airtight container in the refrigerator for up to 4 days.

Country Corn Chowder

Serves 6
30 minutes prep
45 minutes total

One bite of this chowder takes me straight back to wintry Sundays during my childhood. I can almost smell the bacon cooking as I remember watching Mom whip this up after church. Mom learned this recipe from Nana, who regularly had some simmering at the back of her stove for anyone to enjoy on their lunch break. When I was newly married, I wanted to carry this tradition on. But I figured I knew best, and I'd heard of the horrors of bacon fat, so, convinced I was going to improve the recipe (and teach Nana and Mom something), I drained it to make this soup "healthier." I soon realized that I had basically drained all the flavour and created a bland, flat soup. Please learn from my mistake. Close your eyes and keep the bacon fat in the soup pot. Savour its richness, then go for a long Sunday afternoon walk! **Laura**

---

4 cups peeled and cubed russet potatoes
½ tsp salt
4 cobs fresh corn, husked, or 2 cups frozen corn
7 slices bacon, chopped
1 cup diced yellow onion
⅓ cup all-purpose flour
2½ cups milk
1 (14 oz/398 mL) can creamed corn
1 tsp pepper

Place the potatoes in a medium saucepan with just enough water to cover them. Add the salt. Cover and bring to a gentle boil over medium-high heat. Turn down the heat to low and simmer until they are soft but not mushy, about 15 minutes. Do not drain! Set aside.

If you are using fresh corn, bring a large pot of water to a boil over high heat. Add the husked corn cobs to the boiling water. Bring the water back to a rolling boil, then turn off the heat and cover the pot. Let the corn sit in the hot water for 5 minutes before rinsing in very cold water. Cut the kernels off the cobs. Set aside.

In a large pot over medium heat, cook the bacon until the fat is released and the bacon pieces are sizzling and tender, but not browned. Add the onions and cook, stirring occasionally, until the onions are translucent and the bacon is fully cooked, 5–7 minutes.

Sprinkle the flour over the onions and bacon and stir until everything is evenly coated. Slowly add the milk, stirring constantly, and cook until the soup starts to thicken. Turn down the heat to low and simmer for 1 minute.

Pour the potatoes and their water into the soup. Stir in the cooked or frozen corn kernels and creamed corn. Season to taste with the pepper and salt. Warm over medium-low heat until it just starts to bubble, stirring often. Serve hot with crusty bread or biscuits.

Leftovers can be stored in an airtight container in the refrigerator for up to 4 days.

A FARM FAVOURITE

Nana's Beet Borscht

Serves 12
1½ hours prep
3 hours total

Making soup is an art: building layer upon layer of flavours and textures, working toward the final masterpiece. In order to create something truly spectacular, you need to take your time and not rush. Nana understood that. She didn't think twice about devoting her entire morning to making a large pot of this soup, and her door was always open for anyone to come in and have a bowl of it at noon. The secrets to making this soup successfully are deceptively simple: Use good quality ingredients (the mashed potatoes and sautéed cabbage set this soup apart) and follow the instructions to the letter—no cutting corners!

Read through the instructions top to bottom before starting. It's helpful to realize that you will have several pots going at once, with the main pot nicknamed "the soup pot" to help keep the instructions clear. **Rachel**

- 3 medium beets
- 5 Tbsp butter, divided
- 1 medium yellow onion, diced
- 1 can (28 oz/796 mL) diced tomatoes and their juice, or 3 large fresh tomatoes, peeled and chopped
- 7 medium russet potatoes, peeled and cubed, divided
- ¼ cup half-and-half cream
- Salt and pepper
- 8 cups water or chicken broth
- 3 large carrots, diced
- 1 small green cabbage, divided
- ¼ cup fresh dill leaves, chopped, or 2 tsp dried dill weed, plus more to taste
- Sour cream, for serving

Submerge the whole beets in a saucepan of water. Cover and bring to a boil over high heat. Turn down the heat to low and simmer until the beets are cooked through, about 1 hour.

While the beets are cooking, melt 1 Tbsp of the butter in a large stockpot (the soup pot) over medium heat. Add the onions and sauté until translucent, about 5 minutes. Add the tomatoes and their juice. Bring to a light boil and then turn the heat down to low and gently simmer until the tomatoes are soft and the juice is reduced, about 30 minutes. While the tomatoes are simmering, place 4 of the cubed potatoes in a separate stockpot and cover with lightly salted water. Cover and bring to a boil over high heat. Turn down the heat to low and simmer until the potatoes are tender, about 15 minutes. Drain the water. Add 2 Tbsp of the butter, the cream, and a pinch of salt and pepper. Mash with a potato masher until creamy and smooth. Set aside.

Add the water or broth to the soup pot, turn up the heat to medium-high, and bring to a boil. When the soup reaches a boil, add the carrots and turn down the heat to low.

Once the beets are cooked through, place them in cold water. Once they're cool enough to handle, slice the tops off the beets and slip off the skin. It should peel off easily. Chop the beets into ½-inch cubes. Add to the soup pot along with 1 tsp salt and the mashed potatoes, stirring until fully incorporated. Continue to simmer.

In a frying pan over medium heat, melt the remaining 2 Tbsp of butter. Chop half the cabbage into thinly sliced 1-inch »

» strips (you need about 6 cups), add to the frying pan, and sauté, stirring occasionally, until tender, 10–15 minutes. Add to the soup pot with the remaining 3 cubed potatoes.

Chop the remaining cabbage and add it to the soup pot. The soup will be very thick, but remember that the consistency will change as the cabbage softens. If necessary, add more water or broth partway through simmering.

Add the dill, bring to a light boil over medium-high heat, and then turn the heat down to low and simmer the soup, uncovered, until all the vegetables are soft and the flavours have melded, at least 1 hour. Add more dill, salt, or pepper to taste near the end.

Serve with a dollop of sour cream.

Leftovers can be stored in an airtight container in the refrigerator for up to 5 days, or in the freezer for up to 3 months.

Raelene's French Onion Soup

Serves 4
30 minutes prep
2 hours total

Some friends are more like family, as is the case with our dear friend Raelene. Not only did she graciously put up with working alongside us at our farm for more than 20 years, but she also continues to be there for each of us through thick and thin. This recipe is one of her classics. Rich with a deep flavour, it is sure to please. **Tamra**

- 1 Tbsp butter
- 1 Tbsp canola oil
- 8 cups halved and thinly sliced yellow or white onions
- ¼ tsp granulated sugar
- 2 Tbsp all-purpose flour
- 6 cups warm beef broth
- ½ cup white wine
- Salt and pepper
- 4 (½-inch-thick) slices French bread
- 2 tsp olive oil
- 1 clove garlic, crushed
- 1½ cups shredded Swiss cheese

Note: If you don't have time to make the soup all in one day, you can stop after simmering the soup and refrigerate it for up to 4 days. When you are ready to finish the process, simply reheat the soup before putting the bread in the oven. Once the bread has been added, this soup does not store well.

In a large skillet with a lid, warm the butter and oil over medium-low heat. Add the onions and sauté until they are beginning to turn translucent, 5–7 minutes. Stir in the sugar and continue to sauté, stirring frequently, until the onions are golden brown, about 30 minutes. Sprinkle the flour over the onions. Turn up the heat to medium and stir constantly for 2–3 minutes until the flour is evenly dispersed throughout.

Slowly pour in the warm broth and wine, stirring constantly to avoid lumps. Add salt and pepper to taste. Partially cover the pot, turn down the heat to low, and simmer the soup, stirring occasionally, until the onions are cooked soft and the broth has thickened nicely, about 1 hour.

At the 40-minute point, preheat the oven to 400°F.

Place the bread on a baking sheet and toast for 4–5 minutes. Flip the slices over and rub them with the oil and garlic. Toast until golden brown, 4–5 minutes, and then remove from the oven.

Turn the oven down to 325°F. Divide the soup among 4 ovenproof bowls. Sprinkle 2 Tbsp of the cheese into each bowl. Place the bread on top and use the remaining cheese to top the bread in each bowl. Bake until hot and bubbly, 15–20 minutes. Set the oven to broil and, watching closely, broil until the cheese is toasted, 2–3 minutes. Serve immediately.

Cream of Zucchini Soup

Serves 4
15 minutes prep
30 minutes total

This soup is quick to put together, nutritious, and deliciously creamy. We like to eat this for lunch served with crusty bread spread with butter and a slice of cheese. **Tamra**

- 2 Tbsp butter
- ¾ cup diced yellow onion
- 2 cups lightly packed grated zucchini
- 1 cup lightly packed grated carrots
- 2 Tbsp all-purpose flour
- 2 cups chicken broth or water
- 1 cup milk
- Salt and pepper
- 1 cup shredded cheddar cheese

In a Dutch oven or large pot over medium heat, melt the butter. Add the onions and cook until beginning to soften, about 5 minutes. Add the zucchini and carrots and continue to cook, stirring frequently, until the vegetables are softened, 5–10 minutes.

Sprinkle the flour over the vegetables, stirring until fully incorporated. Slowly add the broth or water and the milk, stirring constantly. Bring to a simmer and season to taste with salt and pepper. Turn down the heat to low.

Simmer until the vegetables are fully cooked, about 10 minutes. Add the cheese and stir to melt. Serve immediately.

Leftovers can be stored in an airtight container in the refrigerator for up to 3 days.

A FARM FAVOURITE

Turkey Vegetable Chowder

Serves 8
20 minutes prep
45 minutes total

Second only to a cranberry and turkey sandwich, this chowder is my favourite way to use up leftover turkey. Creamy, loaded with veggies, and full of spices, it has a very well-rounded flavour. Feel free to use chicken in place of turkey for an equally delicious result. **Laura**

- 1 Tbsp canola oil
- 1 medium yellow onion, diced
- 2 cloves garlic, crushed and minced
- 1 tsp dried thyme
- 1 tsp dried basil
- 1 tsp dried oregano
- 8 cups turkey or chicken broth
- 2 cups peeled and cubed russet potatoes
- 1 cup sliced carrots
- 1 stalk celery, including leaves, chopped
- ½–1 tsp salt
- ½ tsp pepper
- 1 cup shredded cheddar cheese
- ¼ cup all-purpose flour
- 2 cups milk
- 4 cups chopped, cooked turkey
- 1½ cups corn kernels, fresh or frozen (see Country Corn Chowder, page 87, if using fresh)
- 1 cup (1-inch pieces) fresh or frozen green beans, or 1 cup fresh or frozen peas

In a large pot, warm the oil over medium heat. Add the onions and sauté until they are almost translucent, 5–7 minutes. Add the garlic and cook until fragrant, about 1 minute. Stir in the thyme, basil, and oregano.

Pour in the broth and increase the heat to medium-high. Add the potatoes, carrots, and celery, cover, and bring to a boil. Add the salt and pepper. Turn down the heat to low and simmer gently, still covered, until the vegetables are tender, 20 minutes.

Stir in the cheese until melted.

In a glass measuring cup, whisk together the flour and milk. Slowly pour this mixture into the pot, stirring constantly. Turn up the heat to medium-low and bring the soup back to a gentle boil for 1 minute.

Stir in the turkey, corn, and beans or peas. Heat through. Taste and adjust the seasonings as needed.

Leftovers can be stored in an airtight container in the refrigerator for up to 4 days or in the freezer for up to 3 months.

Farmhouse Tomato Soup

Serves 6
20 minutes prep
25 minutes total

This soup is, without a doubt, our number one customer favourite at the Farmhouse Café. Not only that, but it is also our most requested recipe! Up until now, we have kept the recipe a farm secret, but we decided that this cookbook would be the perfect opportunity to unveil the recipe for you to enjoy year-round in your own home. **Laura**

- 1 Tbsp butter
- 1 cup diced yellow onions
- 1 (28 oz/796 mL) can diced tomatoes and their juice
- 1 Tbsp fresh dill weed, or 2 tsp dried
- 1½ tsp vegetable bouillon powder
- 2 tsp chopped fresh oregano, or 1 tsp dried
- 1 tsp chopped fresh basil, or ½ tsp dried
- 1 tsp chopped fresh thyme, or ½ tsp dried
- ¾ tsp granulated sugar
- 1 (5½ oz/156 mL) can tomato paste
- Salt
- ½ tsp pepper
- Pinch baking soda
- 1 cup milk
- ¾ cup heavy cream
- Fresh parsley, for garnish (optional)

Melt the butter in a large stockpot over medium heat. Add the onions and sauté, stirring occasionally, until soft and translucent, 5–7 minutes.

Pour in the tomatoes and their juice and bring to a simmer. Add the dill weed, vegetable bouillon, oregano, basil, thyme, and sugar. Return to a boil, turn down the heat to low, and simmer gently, stirring occasionally, until the tomatoes begin to break down, about 15 minutes. If desired, pulse the tomatoes a few times with an immersion blender or mash them with a potato masher to break up remaining large chunks.

Remove from the heat. Stir in the tomato paste, salt to taste, and the pepper. Add a pinch of baking soda to temper the acidity. Slowly pour in the milk and cream, stirring constantly. It is highly likely that your soup will curdle, but don't worry. Add an additional pinch of baking soda and this process will be reversed!

Put the pot back on medium heat and slowly warm the soup through, but do not let it boil. Serve warm, garnishing with fresh parsley if desired.

Leftovers can be stored in an airtight container in the refrigerator for up to 3 days.

A FARM FAVOURITE

Chapter 4

Salads and Sides

Finishing Touches

When I'm planning a meal, I always start by choosing a protein followed by a starch. For example, if I'm making Mini Turkey-Cheddar Meatloaves (page 143), I'll then decide whether we should have potatoes, rice, or pasta alongside it. Unfortunately, that is sometimes where my planning comes to an end. When suppertime rolls around, I am often left scrambling to dream up a side or a salad to balance out the meal. In the summer, this isn't a big problem, as there is fresh produce around every corner, but in the wintertime we sometimes get a little bit tired of steamed peas and carrots.

Compiling this chapter has challenged me to break out of this bad habit. Here you will find a treasure trove of salads, from simple and refreshing to hearty and satisfying, and side dishes that use fresh Canadian ingredients. All it takes is a little bit of planning and foresight to elevate any meal of the week: a lesson I am still learning.

Quite the opposite of me, my mother-in-law, Tamra, is a wizard at balancing out meals, so naturally most of these recipes come from her. Tamra thinks in colour, and as she is planning a meal she keeps this in mind as she weighs all the factors that go into making a delicious and comprehensive spread: Do the flavours go well together? Is there a variety of textures? Will each plate be visually appealing? The result is a beautiful table, laden with a protein, a starch, and a rainbow of sides and salads.

Rachel

Roasted Butternut Squash Salad

Serves 4
15 minutes prep
30 minutes total

Hearty enough to be a full meal, this salad is a celebration of autumn's bounty. Featuring honey-coated roasted squash, dried cranberries, fresh lettuce greens, and an apple-based dressing, the components are the best that an Okanagan autumn has to offer. **Tamra**

Dressing

½ cup Davison Apple Juice
2 Tbsp apple cider vinegar
2 garlic cloves, finely minced
2 tsp cornstarch
¼ tsp dried mustard
5 Tbsp extra virgin olive oil

Salad

½ small butternut squash, peeled, deseeded, and cut into ¼-inch slices
1 Tbsp honey
½ tsp salt
3–4 cups mixed lettuce greens
1 cup crumbled feta cheese
¼ cup pepitas (shelled pumpkin seeds)
¼ cup dried cranberries

Preheat the oven to 400°F. Line a rimmed baking sheet with parchment paper.

For the dressing

In a small saucepan, stir together the apple juice, apple cider vinegar, minced garlic, cornstarch, and dried mustard. Bring to a boil over medium heat, turn down the heat to low, and simmer, stirring frequently, until reduced, 5–7 minutes. Remove from the heat and whisk in the oil. Set aside to cool in the pot.

For the salad

Place the sliced squash on the prepared baking sheet. Brush both sides with the honey and then sprinkle on the salt. Roast until the squash pierces easily with a fork but is still firm enough to hold its shape, 10–12 minutes.

Divide the mixed lettuce greens among 4 salad plates. Top with the warm squash, drizzle on the dressing, and sprinkle on the feta cheese, pepitas, and dried cranberries. Serve immediately.

Showstopper Salad

Serves 12
30 minutes prep
2½ hours total,
plus time to chill the eggs

Our dear friend Heather introduced this eye-catching salad to our family. We now enjoy it at Thanksgiving and other special family meals. Because it needs to be assembled a couple of hours before dinner, it's the perfect salad to take on the road when someone else is hosting the meal. Leftovers are surprisingly good the next day! **Laura**

Salad

- 6 eggs
- 1 head of iceberg lettuce
- 1½ cups frozen peas
- 1 cup chopped bell peppers, any colour (I like a mix of red, yellow, and orange)
- 4 green onions, chopped
- 1 cup chopped celery
- 1½ cups shredded cheddar cheese
- 1 cup fully cooked, crumbled bacon

Dressing

- 1 cup mayonnaise
- 1 cup sour cream
- 2 tsp granulated sugar
- ½ tsp salt

Place the eggs in a large saucepan and cover them with water. Cover the pot with a lid and bring the water to a boil over high heat. Once the water is boiling, turn off the heat and let the eggs sit for 12 minutes. Remove the eggs from the water and chill, either in ice water for 30 minutes or in the refrigerator for at least 2 hours. This step can be done up to 2 days in advance.

For the dressing

To make the dressing, whisk together the mayonnaise, sour cream, sugar, and salt. Set aside. This can be done a day or two in advance, if desired.

For the salad

Wash, pat or spin dry, and shred the lettuce. Place it in a large, deep, glass salad bowl. Layer the frozen peas, peppers, green onions, and celery on top of the lettuce.

Carefully peel the chilled hard-boiled eggs. Slice them into ⅓-inch rounds and lay them on top of the celery.

Pour the dressing carefully and evenly over the salad.

Scatter the cheese and bacon overtop. Cover and refrigerate for at least 2 hours before serving.

Leftovers can be kept in an airtight container in the refrigerator for up to 2 days.

Creamy Dill Cucumber Salad

Serves 6
10 minutes prep
10 minutes total

My children love this creamy, crunchy, refreshing salad. We like to eat it alongside barbecued chicken breasts or hamburgers on summer nights. The dressing can be made a few hours ahead of time, making the salad very quick to throw together! If your cucumbers release water before you dress them, drain the excess moisture and pat them dry with a paper towel. **Rachel**

¼ cup sour cream
¼ cup mayonnaise
2 tsp lemon juice
1–2 tsp fresh or dried dill weed
¼ tsp granulated sugar
3 field cucumbers
¼ tsp salt

In a small bowl, whisk together the sour cream, mayonnaise, lemon juice, dill weed, and sugar. Cover and refrigerate until you are ready to assemble the salad (up to 12 hours ahead of time).

Peel and thinly slice the cucumbers. Place them in a bowl and sprinkle with the salt. Mix thoroughly.

Pour the dressing over the cucumbers. Mix well and garnish with fresh dill. This salad is best served immediately, but leftovers can be kept in an airtight container in the refrigerator for up to 2 days. Note, though, that the cucumbers will lose their crunch if they sit in the dressing for any length of time.

DAV

Stoplight Salad

Serves 5 as a main,
10 as a side
25 minutes prep
25 minutes total

I only make this salad in the summertime when fresh corn and field-ripened tomatoes are available. If you are desperate to make it in the colder months, use cherry tomatoes, as they tend to have the best flavour out of season, and canned corn. For a lighter, more traditional version, omit the quinoa. Leftovers are amazing in a wrap paired with shredded cheddar cheese and/or grilled chicken. **Laura**

Salad

- 2 cobs fresh corn, husked, or 1 (12 oz/341 mL) can corn, drained
- 1 (19 oz/540 mL) can black beans, drained and rinsed
- 2 cups chopped field tomatoes or quartered cherry tomatoes
- 2 cups cooked quinoa (see note)
- 2 cups chopped coloured bell peppers (I like an assortment of red, green, and orange)
- ¼ cup chopped green onions, whites included
- ¼ cup chopped cilantro

Dressing

- ¼ cup freshly squeezed lime juice (about 2 limes)
- ¼ cup extra virgin olive oil
- 1 tsp salt
- 1 tsp minced garlic

Note: To cook the quinoa, simply follow the package instructions and let cool before adding to the prepared vegetables.

For the salad

If you're using fresh corn, bring a large pot of salted water to a boil over high heat. Add the husked corncobs to the pot. Bring the water back to a rolling boil, then turn off the heat and cover the pot. Let the corn sit in the hot water for 5 minutes before rinsing in very cold water. Cut the kernels off the cobs (or, if using canned corn, drain the liquid from the kernels) and place them in a large bowl.

Add the black beans, tomatoes, quinoa, peppers, green onions, and cilantro to the bowl. Toss to combine.

For the dressing

In a glass measuring cup, whisk together the lime juice, oil, salt, and minced garlic. Pour this dressing over the vegetables and stir to combine. Serve immediately.

Leftovers can be stored in an airtight container in the refrigerator for up to 3 days.

Tamra's Pasta Salad

Serves 6
15 minutes prep
25 minutes total, plus chilling

Simple yet completely delicious, this summertime salad has been a staple in the Davison household for as long as anyone can remember. Laura and I typically make ours without the cucumber, whereas Rachel likes to add it for some crunch and colour. This is our favourite salad to bring to summer potlucks. **Tamra**

---

4 cups dry rotini noodles
½ tsp salt
1½ cups chopped tomatoes
1 cup peeled and chopped field cucumber (optional)
⅓ cup freshly grated parmesan cheese
¼ cup chopped fresh basil leaves
½ cup Caesar salad dressing (use your favourite)

Bring a large pot of water to a rolling boil over high heat. Add the pasta and salt. Cook until al dente, about 7–10 minutes. Drain the pasta into a colander and rinse well with cold water. Transfer to a large salad bowl. Cover and chill in the refrigerator for at least 30 minutes and up to 24 hours.

When you are ready to serve, add the tomatoes, cucumbers (if using), parmesan, and basil. Toss well to combine. Pour the dressing over everything and toss to coat. Serve immediately.

Store leftovers in an airtight container in the refrigerator for up to 2 days.

Tzatziki Sauce

2½ cups
15 minutes prep
1–2 hours total, plus chilling

A freshly picked field cucumber and local garlic make all the difference in this recipe. We enjoy this as a dip for cut-up vegetables or pita bread, on top of Zucchini Pancakes (page 61), or alongside any chicken dish. **Rachel**

- 1 large fresh field or English cucumber
- ½ tsp salt, divided
- 2 Tbsp fresh dill weed, or 1 Tbsp dried
- 1–2 tsp minced garlic
- 2 cups thick, plain Greek yogurt
- 2 Tbsp freshly squeezed lemon juice

Peel the cucumber and slice it in half lengthwise. Scoop out and discard the seeds and pulp. Grate the cucumber and stir in ¼ tsp of the salt. Transfer to a colander set inside a bowl and put aside to drain at room temperature for at least 30 minutes and up to 2 hours. Pat the drained cucumber with a paper towel to pull out any remaining liquid.

In a medium bowl, stir together the drained cucumber, dill weed, garlic, the remaining ¼ tsp of salt, the yogurt, and the lemon juice. Cover and chill for at least 3 hours and up to 12 hours before serving to allow the flavours to meld. Stir before serving.

Store leftovers in an airtight container in the refrigerator for up to 2 days.

Apple Baked Squash

Serves 6
30 minutes prep
2 hours total

This exceptional side dish is found on our tables only two times a year: Christmas Day and Thanksgiving Day. But if you want to eat it weekly, we won't judge! **Tamra**

- 1 medium butternut squash, peeled, deseeded, and cut into ¼-inch-thick slices
- 2–3 apples, peeled, cored, halved, and cut into ¼-inch-thick slices (see note)
- ⅓ cup brown sugar, lightly packed
- ⅓ cup butter, softened
- 2 tsp all-purpose flour
- ½ tsp salt
- ⅓ tsp ground cinnamon

Note: Our favourite apples to use in this dish are Mutsu, Honeycrisp, Spartan, or Golden Delicious.

Preheat the oven to 375°F. Lightly grease an 8 × 8-inch baking dish.

Place the squash slices in the prepared dish (it's fine if they overlap). Arrange the apple slices over the top of the squash.

In a small mixing bowl, beat together the sugar, butter, flour, salt, and cinnamon until smooth. Drop this mixture by spoonfuls over the apples.

Cover with aluminum foil and bake until the squash is fork-tender and everything is bubbly, about 1 hour and 15 minutes. Serve hot.

Leftovers can be stored in an airtight container in the refrigerator for up to 4 days.

Basil and Feta Tomatoes

Serves 6
5 minutes prep
5 minutes total

Before my mom (Tamra) married a farmer, she studied fashion and interior design at college. She is the mastermind behind the colours, design, and decor at the farm. This side dish is as beautiful as it is delicious, and sometimes I wonder if Mom puts it on the table to enjoy the visual feast just as much as the edible one. **Laura**

- 3 large field tomatoes, sliced ¼ inch thick
- ½ cup crumbled feta cheese
- 6 basil leaves, chopped
- 3 Tbsp balsamic reduction

Arrange the tomato slices on a large platter. Sprinkle the cheese and basil overtop.

Right before serving, drizzle the balsamic reduction over the tomatoes. They can be served alongside just about anything.

These do not keep well, but that's never a problem because they always get devoured!

Bacon-Wrapped Jalapeños

8 jalapeño halves
20 minutes prep
60 minutes total

Three simple ingredients, a little bit of patience and a few minutes in the oven will produce a party favourite. Unless you're only cooking for two, you're going to want to make more than eight of these beauties. We guarantee that everyone will be looking for more. For an extra bite, top with freshly ground black pepper. **Laura**

- 4 jalapeño peppers, sliced in half lengthwise and deseeded
- 4 strips bacon, sliced in half lengthwise
- 1 (8 oz/250 g) package cream cheese

Preheat the oven to 400°F. Line a rimmed baking sheet with parchment paper.

Cut the cream cheese into 8 evenly sized slices. Stuff each slice of cream cheese into a jalapeño half. Wrap the bacon halves around the stuffed jalapeños. Secure with a toothpick. Place on the prepared baking sheet.

Bake until the cream cheese is hot and bubbly and the bacon is crispy, 30–40 minutes. Serve hot from the oven, either as an appetizer or a fun side dish.

Chapter 5

Mains

Everyday Wisdom

Dora Davison, known by everyone as Nana, is one of the hardest-working people I know. She had a happy childhood, but times were difficult and her family worked diligently to make ends meet. In early adulthood she married Bob Davison and adapted easily to farm life. Money was scarce, but with ingenuity and positivity they raised six children and always had food on the table.

I love to talk to Nana about those days. Sometimes I've asked her how she did it. How did she raise the kids, grow a garden, make everything from scratch, work in the orchard, balance the books, volunteer at church, and on and on? Her simple answer is one we can all learn from: "When I get up in the morning, I make my bed. Then I do the breakfast dishes and plan out what we are going to have for supper. After that, I am free to enjoy the rest of my day."

How basic and yet revolutionary! As I write this, Nana is 93 years of age and still following this routine. It hasn't failed her yet. Making the bed signifies the start of a new day that has order and purpose. Doing the dishes keeps the counters, and therefore the mind, free of mess and clutter. And planning the main meal allows the day to go smoothly without the stress that comes with last-minute scrambling.

In this chapter you will find fresh inspiration to tackle planning your meals after your bed is made and the dishes are put away. From Nana's, Tamra's, Laura's, and my kitchens, these main dishes will satisfy whether you are looking for comfort food, something simple, or something to impress. With an emphasis on eating seasonally, there is something here for every occasion and every time of year.

Rachel

Delicata Squash Pot Pie

Serves 8
45 minutes prep
1 hour, 30 minutes total

There are a few reasons I like this one-pot meal. First of all, the dumplings, which are nothing short of a delicacy, are the ultimate old-fashioned comfort food. Second, the stew is loaded with veggies that can be found in the average Canadian garden. How wonderful to make a hearty meal with all local ingredients. And third, it takes less than an hour's hands-on time to make, which is manageable for a weeknight supper. **Laura**

Stew

- 1 Delicata squash (see note)
- 1 lb sausage of your choice, casings removed (I like to use Davison Apple Cider Sausage)
- 1 cup diced white onion
- 3 cloves garlic, crushed and minced
- 1 tsp dried rosemary
- 1 tsp dried thyme
- 3 carrots, chopped
- 1 red bell pepper, deseeded and diced
- 1 green bell pepper, deseeded and diced
- 2 Tbsp all-purpose flour
- 4 cups chicken broth
- 2–3 cups (1-inch cubes) red or yellow potatoes
- 1 tsp salt
- ½ tsp pepper

Dumplings

- 1¾ cups all-purpose flour
- 2½ tsp baking powder
- ½ tsp salt
- ⅓ cup cold butter or margarine, cubed
- Milk
- Parsley leaves, for garnish (optional)

For the stew

Cut the squash in half lengthwise and scrape out all the seeds. Place one half of the squash in a microwave-safe dish with 1 Tbsp of water in the bottom. Microwave on high until the flesh is cooked and soft, 7–10 minutes. Set aside to cool. You will use this in the dumplings. Peel and chop the other half of the squash into ½-inch cubes. Set aside for the stew.

In a Dutch oven set over medium-high heat, cook the sausage and onion, crumbling the sausage with a wooden spoon, until it is fully cooked, about 5 minutes. Add the garlic, rosemary, and thyme and cook just until the garlic begins to soften, about 1 minute.

Stir in the carrots and peppers. Sprinkle on the flour and stir well to distribute it evenly. Slowly pour in the broth, stirring constantly. Bring to a boil and then turn down the heat to medium. Add the potatoes, cubed squash, salt, and pepper. Bring to a gentle boil, turn down the heat to low, cover the pot, and simmer until the vegetables are tender, 16–20 minutes.

For the dumplings

Preheat the oven to 425°F.

In a large bowl, whisk together the flour, baking powder, and salt. Using a pastry blender, a fork, or your hands, cut in the butter until the mixture resembles coarse crumbs. The butter pieces should be no larger than a pea. Alternatively, pulse the dry ingredients and the butter in a food processor fitted with the steel blade. Scoop the cooked squash into a glass measuring cup. Add enough milk to bring the measurement to 1¼ cups. Mix until well combined. Pour over the flour mixture. Stir gently, just enough to combine. »

Note: A Delicata squash is a small, oblong squash that ranges in colour from yellow to orange to tan and has green or orange stripes. It has a mild flavour and the flesh is a pale yellow. If you can't find one in your area, acorn squash makes a good substitute.

» Drop the dough by spoonfuls onto the simmering stew, making 8 evenly sized dumplings. Cover with a lid and bake undisturbed for 15 minutes. Remove from the oven, uncover, and let stand for 5–10 minutes before serving. The dumplings should bounce back when pressed lightly with a spoon. Garnish with minced parsley leaves, if desired.

Leftovers can be stored in an airtight container in the refrigerator for up to 3 days.

DAVISON
ORCHARDS

Summer in a Pan

Serves 4
30 minutes prep
1 hour total

Sheet pan suppers are wonderful recipes to have in your repertoire. Throwing everything onto one pan and letting it bake is simple and quick—and the cleanup couldn't be easier! This dish uses local ingredients that are in season at the peak of summer. My favourite way to use leftovers is to make a breakfast skillet by frying them in a pan and scrambling in eggs. **Rachel**

- 6 small red or yellow potatoes, quartered
- 1 white onion, halved and sliced
- 4 cloves garlic, peeled and left whole
- 2 Tbsp olive oil, divided
- ½ tsp seasoning salt, divided
- 1 tsp lemon pepper, divided
- ¾ cup cherry tomatoes
- 2 small zucchinis, halved lengthwise and sliced into ½-inch semicircles
- 1 poblano pepper, roughly chopped
- 4–6 fresh basil leaves, chopped or torn
- 1 lb sausages of your choice (I like to use Davison Apple Cider Sausage)

Preheat the oven to 375°F. Line a rimmed baking sheet with parchment paper.

Place the potatoes, onions, and garlic in a bowl. Drizzle with 1 Tbsp of the oil and toss to coat. Season with half of the salt and half of the pepper. Place on the prepared baking pan and bake for 15 minutes.

Meanwhile, place the tomatoes, zucchini, and poblano pepper in the same bowl you used for the root vegetables. Toss with the remaining oil, salt and pepper.

After the root vegetables have baked for 15 minutes, stir them. Add the other vegetables to the pan and spread them all around evenly. Sprinkle on the basil. Nestle the sausages on top and return to the oven until the vegetables are tender and the sausage has reached an internal temperature of 160°F, 20–25 minutes.

Leftovers can be stored in an airtight container in the refrigerator for up to 3 days.

Grilled Chicken with Strawberry Salsa

Serves 4
45 minutes prep
45 minutes total, plus marinating

The salsa in this recipe was developed by my sister Leah and our long-time food service manager and friend Raelene. It was originally served in the Farmhouse Café on grilled focaccia with brie. It is simple and yet both stunning and delicious. It's a real spring treat and the perfect match for grilled chicken. **Laura**

Grilled Chicken

¼ cup olive oil
¼ cup freshly squeezed lemon juice (2–3 lemons)
1 clove garlic, minced
1 tsp dried basil
½ tsp salt
¼ tsp pepper
4 boneless skinless chicken breasts

Strawberry Salsa

3½ cups diced fresh strawberries, hulled (about 2 pints whole)
4 tsp olive oil
2 tsp balsamic reduction, plus more for serving
2 tsp balsamic vinegar
2 tsp chopped fresh basil
1 tsp lime zest
¼ tsp salt
¼ tsp pepper
Arugula, for serving (optional)
Cooked rice, for serving

For the chicken

In a glass measuring cup, whisk together the oil, lemon juice, garlic, basil, salt, and pepper. Place the chicken breasts in a shallow container and pour the marinade overtop. Cover and refrigerate for at least 30 minutes, or up to 24 hours.

For the salsa

Toss the strawberries with the oil, balsamic reduction, balsamic vinegar, basil, lime zest, salt, and pepper until well combined. Set aside until ready to serve. (Don't make this too far ahead of time.)

To cook the chicken

Preheat the barbecue to about 400°F.

Grill the chicken, flipping every 5 minutes, until the internal temperature has just reached 165°F, 15–17 minutes. Remove from the grill, cover with aluminum foil, and let rest for 5 minutes before serving.

Generously pile each chicken breast with strawberry salsa. Top with a handful of arugula (if using) and a drizzle of balsamic reduction (if using). Serve with rice.

Picnic Chicken

Serves 6
15 minutes prep
1 hour, 15 minutes total

For many years we opened up our orchard on Mother's Day for people to enjoy a picnic, made by us, under the blossoming apple trees. This chicken recipe was the main dish on the menu and was always much enjoyed. **Tamra**

- 1 egg
- 2 Tbsp water
- 1 Tbsp dried basil
- 2 tsp salt
- ½ tsp pepper
- 12 chicken drumsticks and/or thighs, skin on
- 2 cups fine bread crumbs
- 2 Tbsp butter, melted
- 1 Tbsp fresh parsley, chopped

Preheat the oven to 400°F. Coat a baking pan with cooking spray or line it with parchment paper.

In a bowl, lightly whisk together the egg and water. Stir in the basil, salt, and pepper. Drop the chicken into the egg mixture and swish and stir until the chicken is well coated.

Place the bread crumbs in a shallow dish. Liberally coat the chicken in crumbs. Place on the prepared pan. Drizzle the melted butter over the chicken.

Bake, uncovered, until the chicken has reached an internal temperature of 165°F, about 1 hour. Sprinkle with parsley before serving. This is great served hot or cold!

Leftovers can be stored in an airtight container in the refrigerator for up to 2 days.

Okanagan Baked Chicken

Serves 4
30 minutes prep
1 hour, 15 minutes total

Juicy peaches, sumptuous chicken, tangy sweet and sour sauce—this supper is a celebration of an Okanagan summer. After a day out on the lake or hiking the mountain trails, this really hits the spot. **Tamra**

- ¼ cup all-purpose flour
- 1 tsp salt
- 4 boneless, skinless chicken breasts
- 2 Tbsp butter
- ¼ cup brown sugar, lightly packed
- 1 Tbsp cornstarch
- ½ cup orange juice
- ¼ cup white vinegar
- 2 Tbsp soy sauce
- 1 Tbsp lemon juice
- 3 fresh peaches, peeled, stones removed, and sliced (or 2½ cups canned sliced peaches, well drained)
- ¾ cup thinly sliced white onion
- 1 red bell pepper, thinly sliced
- Cooked rice, for serving

Preheat the oven to 350°F. Coat a glass casserole dish large enough to hold the chicken without crowding with cooking spray.

In a shallow bowl, mix together the flour and salt. Dredge each chicken breast in the flour mixture, coating both sides. Shake off any excess flour.

In a skillet over medium-high heat, melt the butter. Brown the chicken on both sides, about 5 minutes per side. Place the browned chicken in the prepared casserole dish.

In the same skillet, combine the sugar, cornstarch, orange juice, vinegar, soy sauce, and lemon juice. Whisk together and warm over medium, stirring constantly, until the mixture thickens and coats the back of your spoon. Be sure to scrape up any browned bits left from the chicken!

Layer the peaches, followed by the onions and then the bell peppers, over the chicken. Pour the sauce evenly overtop of everything. Cover with aluminum foil and bake until the internal temperature of the chicken is 165°F, about 45 minutes.

Serve hot over rice.

Leftovers can be stored in an airtight container in the refrigerator for up to 3 days.

Mini Turkey-Cheddar Meatloaves

Serves 6
20 minutes prep
1 hour, 20 minutes total

Not only are these mini meatloaves delicious with just about every side dish I can think of, but they also make for a brilliant meatloaf sandwich if you're lucky enough to have leftovers. Ground beef is just as good as ground turkey, so use whichever suits your mood. **Rachel**

Meatloaves

- 1 egg
- ½ cup milk
- ¾ cup shredded old cheddar cheese
- ½ cup quick oats
- ½ cup minced yellow onion
- 1 tsp salt
- 1 lb ground turkey

Sauce

- 1 (5½ oz/156 mL) can tomato paste
- 2 Tbsp ketchup
- 2 Tbsp white vinegar
- 1 Tbsp brown sugar
- 1 tsp dried mustard

Preheat the oven to 350°F. Coat a 9 × 13-inch baking dish with cooking spray or line it with parchment paper. Set aside.

For the meatloaves

In a large bowl, whisk together the egg and milk. Add the cheese, oats, onions, and salt. Stir to combine and allow to sit at room temperature for 5 minutes. Add the ground turkey and stir to just combine. Using a ½-cup measuring cup, scoop up and shape the meat into 6 loaves, placing them in the prepared dish.

For the sauce

In a small bowl, stir together the tomato paste, ketchup, vinegar, sugar, and dried mustard. Spoon the sauce onto the loaves, dividing it equally. Spread the sauce with the back of the spoon over the tops so each loaf is covered.

Bake, uncovered, until the internal temperature of the middle loaf is 165°F (160°F if you're using ground beef), about 1 hour. Serve immediately.

Store leftovers in an airtight container in the refrigerator for up to 3 days.

Beef Stew

Serves 8
1 hour prep
7–9 hours total

Beef stew paired with flaky biscuits (see page 31) is one of my favourite suppers in the late autumn and winter months. If you don't have a squash on hand or you just don't like squash, simply omit it and add a few more potatoes or carrots to make up the difference. **Rachel**

---

1 Tbsp olive oil
1½ lb stewing beef
1 large yellow onion, diced
4 cloves garlic, crushed and minced
Salt and pepper
1 (28 oz/796 mL) can diced tomatoes and their juice
¾ cup beef broth, plus more if needed
1 cup (¾-inch pieces) celery ribs and leaves, cut on the diagonal
2 cups (¾-inch pieces) carrots, cut on the diagonal
3 large russet or white potatoes, peeled and cut into 1-inch cubes
2 cups (¾-inch cubes) squash, peeled and deseeded (butternut or Delicata works well)
3 bay leaves
½ tsp dried basil
½ tsp garlic powder
2 Tbsp cornstarch
2 Tbsp cold water
1 cup (1-inch pieces) fresh or frozen green beans

Note: If you don't have a slow cooker, you can add all the vegetables and spices to the Dutch oven and simmer slowly on the stovetop for about 1 hour, 30 minutes, or bake in the oven at 300°F for 3½–4 hours.

In a Dutch oven or heavy skillet with a lid, warm the oil over medium heat. Add the beef, onions, and garlic and fry until the beef is browned on all sides. Season the beef with salt and pepper while it's browning.

Once the meat is browned, add the tomatoes and their juice and the broth. Bring to a boil, turn down the heat to low, cover the pot with a lid, and simmer gently, stirring occasionally, for 45 minutes. If your liquid reduces below your meat, add more broth to keep the meat covered.

Place all the vegetables (except the green beans) in the slow cooker.

Carefully pour the meat mixture over the vegetables and add the spices. Stir gently to combine.

Cook on low for 8 hours, or on high for 6 hours.

About 1 hour before you plan to serve your meal, mix together the cornstarch and cold water in a small bowl. Slowly add to the stew, stirring constantly. Fold in the green beans. Cover and continue cooking for another hour.

Serve with Nana's Cheese Biscuits (page 31).

Store leftovers in an airtight container in the refrigerator for up to 4 days.

Nana's Meat Pie

Serves 8
35 minutes prep
4½ hours total, plus cooling and time to prep the pastry

As is fitting given our British heritage, this meat pie has been a staple in our family for generations. Served with buttery mashed potatoes and pickled beets, this is comfort food at its finest. When Nana's grandchildren started leaving home it was not unusual for them to find a meat pie or two on the passenger seat of their cars after they visited her. No college student in her family was going to be living off frozen pizzas if she could help it! When I asked her for the recipe, she was quite surprised: "Recipe? Just stew some beef and bake it in a pastry." Hmm. Thanks, Nana. After some trial and error, mixed with a lot of nagging for more information, we were able to re-create the pie that transported us back to Nana's kitchen. Here it is, finally, in writing, so that you too can enjoy this classic British dish. **Rachel**

- 3 lb beef (chuck beef, round steak, or stewing beef works well)
- ¾ cup all-purpose flour
- 2 Tbsp butter
- 2½ cups water, plus more if needed
- 2 cloves garlic, quartered
- 2 Tbsp dried onion flakes
- 1 Tbsp beef bouillon powder
- ¼ tsp paprika
- ¼ tsp celery seed
- Salt and pepper
- ¼ batch Homemade Pie Dough (page 171)

To prepare the beef filling

Preheat the oven to 350°F.

Cut the beef into 1-inch cubes, trimming the fat as needed. Place the flour in a shallow bowl. Dredge the beef in the flour to coat it.

In a heavy skillet with a lid, or a large Dutch oven, melt the butter over medium heat. Brown the beef, stirring regularly, until golden on each side, about 7 minutes in total. Add the water to the skillet and stir, scraping the bottom to loosen the browned bits. Add the garlic and spices and stir to combine.

Cover with a lid and bake until the meat is fall-apart tender, at least 2 hours. Stir it every hour or so. If the meat is getting dry during the cooking process, add more water to cover it. Your filling is ready when the meat is fork-tender and the gravy is thick and dark brown.

Remove the lid and let the meat filling cool on the counter for 20 minutes. Transfer to the refrigerator and let cool completely, about 2 more hours. You can prepare the meat a day or two in advance, which allows for overnight cooling and improved flavour.

To assemble the pie

Preheat the oven to 350°F.

Divide the dough in half. Roll out one half of the dough to a 12-inch circle. Gently fit it into a deep 9-inch pie plate, trimming off any excess. Set aside. Roll out the dough for your lid, just as you did for the bottom. Set aside.
Spread the meat into the pie shell. »

» It will be thick when cold! Gently place the reserved circle of dough over the top, trimming the excess to ¼ inch from the edge of the plate. Tuck the extra ¼ inch of dough under the lip of the dough in the bottom of the dish. Crimp to seal with your fingers or with a fork. Cut a venting hole in whatever shape you like in the centre of your top crust.

Bake until golden brown, 60–75 minutes. Let stand for 10 minutes before serving.

Leftovers can be stored in an airtight container in the refrigerator for up to 4 days.

Sweet Potato Shepherd's Pie

Serves 6
35 minutes prep
1 hour total

Beef and vegetables bubbling in thick gravy, buried under a mountain of creamy mashed russet and sweet potatoes: pure bliss! **Rachel**

Topping

- 3 russet potatoes, peeled and cut into 1½-inch cubes (about 4 cups)
- ½ tsp salt, plus more to taste
- 1 medium sweet potato, peeled and cut into 1-inch cubes (about 2½ cups)
- ¼ cup + 2 Tbsp freshly grated parmesan cheese, divided
- ¼ cup butter
- ¼ cup sour cream
- ¼ tsp pepper

Filling

- 1½ lb extra-lean ground beef
- 1 yellow onion, diced
- 2 tsp crushed and minced garlic
- 1 cup peeled and chopped carrots
- 1 tsp paprika
- ½ tsp dried thyme
- ¾ tsp salt
- ½ tsp pepper
- 1 cup peas, frozen or fresh
- ½ cup (1-inch pieces) fresh or frozen green beans
- 1 cup beef broth
- 2 Tbsp ketchup
- 1 Tbsp Worcestershire sauce
- 2 Tbsp all-purpose flour

For the topping

Place the russet potatoes in a large pot and cover them with water. Bring to a boil over high heat. Add the ½ tsp salt and then the sweet potatoes. Cover and cook over medium-low heat until tender, 12–14 minutes. Drain. Add the ¼ cup of parmesan cheese, the butter, sour cream, pepper, and salt to taste to the potatoes. Mash until smooth and creamy.

For the filling

Preheat the oven to 375°F.

Place the ground beef and onions in a heavy, ovenproof skillet and cook over medium heat until no longer pink. Add the garlic and carrots and keep cooking until the meat is nicely browned and the carrots are beginning to soften, about 5 minutes. Stir in the paprika, thyme, salt, and pepper. Cook for 1 minute, just to combine the flavours. Mix in the peas and beans.

In a glass measuring cup, mix together the broth, ketchup, and Worcestershire sauce. Sprinkle the flour over the beef mixture, stirring until fully incorporated. Slowly pour the broth mixture over the meat, stirring to avoid lumps. Cook on medium heat, stirring frequently, until hot and bubbly, about 5–7 minutes. Adjust the seasonings to taste.

Top with the mashed potatoes and sprinkle the remaining 2 Tbsp of parmesan cheese overtop.

Bake, uncovered, until hot and bubbly, about 25 minutes. Let stand for 10 minutes before serving.

Store leftovers in an airtight container in the refrigerator for up to 4 days.

A FARM FAVOURITE

Hearty Chili and Cornbread Casserole

Serves 8
40 minutes prep
1½ hours total

Chili is such a satisfying comfort food on a blustery day. This recipe combines the chili and the cornbread into one dish, making it a one-pot wonder. It works just as well if you keep them separate, though (see note), so the choice is yours. **Laura**

Chili

- 1½ lb lean ground beef
- 1 medium yellow onion, diced
- 3 cloves garlic, crushed and minced
- 1 green bell pepper, deseeded and chopped
- 1 stalk celery, chopped
- 1 (28 oz/796 mL) can diced tomatoes and their juice
- ⅓ cup ketchup
- 1 Tbsp white vinegar
- 1 Tbsp brown sugar
- 2½ Tbsp chili powder
- ½ tsp dried mustard
- ¾ tsp salt
- ½ tsp pepper
- 1 can (14 oz/398 mL) brown beans in tomato sauce
- 1 can (19 oz/540 mL) black beans, drained and rinsed
- 1 can (19 oz/540 mL) kidney beans, drained and rinsed

Cornbread Topper

- ¾ cup cornmeal
- 1¼ cups milk
- 1 egg
- ¼ cup canola oil
- 1 cup all-purpose flour
- ¼ cup granulated sugar
- 1 Tbsp baking powder
- ½ tsp salt

For the chili

Warm a large Dutch oven over medium heat. Add the ground beef and onions and cook, crumbling the meat with a wooden spoon, until the meat is browned and the onion is clear, 5–7 minutes. Season the beef with a little salt and pepper while it browns.

Add the garlic, bell peppers, and celery and let cook until the vegetables are softened, about 5 minutes.

Stir in the tomatoes and their juice, the ketchup, vinegar, and sugar and bring to a simmer. Add the chili powder, dried mustard, salt, and pepper and stir to combine. Add all the beans.

Partially cover, bring to a simmer, then turn down the heat to medium-low and simmer, stirring occasionally, for 30 minutes. Taste and adjust seasonings as desired partway through cooking. »

Note: If you would rather keep your chili and cornbread separate, pour the batter into a greased 8 × 8-inch baking dish and bake at 375°F until the cornbread is nicely browned and a toothpick inserted into the centre comes out clean, 25–30 minutes. The cornbread can be stored in an airtight container at room temperature for up to 2 days when cooked separately like this. Cook the chili according to the method above.

For the cornbread topper
Preheat the oven to 375°F.

In a large bowl, stir together the cornmeal and milk. Let stand for 10 minutes. Add the egg and oil and stir to combine. In a separate bowl, whisk together the flour, sugar, baking powder, and salt. Add to the cornmeal mixture and stir to just combine.

Carefully pour the batter over the hot chili. Bake, uncovered, until the cornbread is nicely browned and a toothpick inserted into the centre comes out clean, about 25 minutes. Serve immediately. Leftovers can be stored in an airtight container in the refrigerator for up to 3 days, but note that the cornbread can get a little soggy.

Spaghetti Squash Lasagna

Serves 6
20 minutes prep
1 hour, 45 minutes total

One hot and hectic day, I was scrambling to put something together for a backyard family potluck that was happening that night. Looking at what I had on hand, I decided to layer spaghetti squash and meat sauce into a lasagna. When my cousin asked for the recipe, I wrote down what I'd done—and the rest is history. This is now our most popular family recipe on our YouTube channel. **Rachel**

- 1 large spaghetti squash, halved lengthwise, seeds and fibrous strands removed
- ⅔ lb extra-lean ground beef
- ½ cup diced yellow onion
- 1 green bell pepper, chopped
- Salt and pepper
- ½ cup chopped zucchini
- 1½ cups Loads of Herbs Tomato Sauce (page 245) or your favourite store-bought tomato sauce
- 1½ cups cottage cheese
- 2 cups shredded mozzarella cheese

Preheat the oven to 375°F. Line a rimmed baking sheet with parchment paper. Grease an 8 × 8 × 2½-inch baking dish. Cover a baking sheet with aluminum foil and place the baking dish on it to catch any of the contents that bubble over.

Place the spaghetti squash halves cut side down on the prepared baking sheet that is lined with parchment. Bake until soft, about 45 minutes. Lower the oven temperature to 350°F.

In a skillet over medium heat, cook the ground beef, onions, and bell peppers until the meat is almost cooked through, 5–7 minutes. Season to taste with salt and pepper. Add the zucchini and continue cooking until the meat is no longer pink and the vegetables are tender, 5–7 minutes more. Stir in the tomato sauce and bring to a gentle boil. Remove from the heat.

To assemble the lasagna, spread half of the meat mixture over the bottom of the prepared baking dish. Using a fork, pull the flesh out of one of the squash shells and spread it over the meat. Season to taste with salt and pepper. Spread the cottage cheese over the squash, followed by the remainder of the meat. Spread the flesh of the remaining squash half over the top.

Cover the lasagna with aluminum foil and bake until hot and bubbly, about 45 minutes. Remove the foil and sprinkle on the mozzarella cheese. Return to the oven, uncovered, and bake for 5 minutes more, just to melt the cheese. If you enjoy your cheese toasted, set the lasagna under the broiler, keeping a close eye on it until the cheese is browned, 3–4 minutes.

Let the lasagna stand for 15–20 minutes before serving to allow time for it to set.

Store leftovers in an airtight container in the refrigerator for up to 3 days.

Mom's Lazy Cabbage Rolls

Serves 8
20 minutes prep
2 hours, 20 minutes total

Cabbage rolls are one of those dishes that I absolutely love but never make. They are just too fiddly to put together! This casserole is the perfect solution. It is very easy to throw together and still has the authentic flavour of traditional cabbage rolls. When I was first married, I made a similar casserole for my husband. After a few bites he politely suggested that I ask his mother for her recipe. When my wounded pride had recovered I did just that. And am I ever glad I did! So, here it is for you to get it right the first time: Mom's Lazy Cabbage Rolls. **Rachel**

1½ lb lean ground beef
2 medium yellow onions, diced
1 clove garlic, crushed and minced
½–1 tsp salt
½ tsp pepper
1 (28 oz/796 mL) can diced tomatoes and their juice
1 (9.6 oz/284 mL) can condensed tomato soup
½ cup water
½ cup uncooked long-grain rice
6 cups shredded green cabbage

In a Dutch oven over medium heat, cook the ground beef and onions until the meat is no longer pink, 5–7 minutes. Add the garlic, salt, and pepper and cook until fragrant, about 2 minutes more.

Pour in the tomatoes and their juice, the soup, and the water. Bring to a simmer, still over medium heat, stirring occasionally. Stir in the rice, return to a simmer, and then turn down the heat to maintain a gentle simmer. Cover with a lid and simmer, stirring occasionally, until the rice is just cooked, about 20 minutes.

Preheat the oven to 350°F. Grease a 9 × 13-inch casserole dish.

Place half of the cabbage in the prepared casserole dish. Spread half of the meat mixture over the cabbage. Repeat with the remaining cabbage and meat.

Cover with aluminum foil and bake until the cabbage is soft and the liquid is mostly absorbed, about 1½ hours. Let stand for 10 minutes before serving.

Serve with a dollop of sour cream, if desired. We always eat this with a side of perogies, pickled beets (page 235), and steamed peas and carrots.

Store leftovers in an airtight container in the refrigerator for up to 4 days. You can also freeze the baked casserole for up to 4 months. Thaw in the refrigerator overnight and reheat in the oven at 350°F for approximately 1 hour.

Stuffed Peppers

Serves 6
25 minutes prep
1 hour, 10 minutes total

This is a classic Davison Family recipe. When the first bell peppers are beginning to ripen in our fields, I cook up a massive batch of this meat filling. Then I freeze it in bags to pull out for quick and delicious meals any night of the week. Because this recipe is a little outdated, we thought about tweaking it to make it more contemporary. But these peppers have been such a staple at all of our dinner tables for so many years that we decided to keep it authentic. So, embrace the 1990s and enjoy! These are delicious with Basil and Feta Tomatoes (page 121), corn on the cob, and focaccia. **Tamra**

½ cup long-grain white rice
1 lb lean ground beef
½ cup diced yellow onion
1 (9.6 oz/284 mL) can condensed tomato soup
2 tsp Worcestershire sauce
½ tsp salt
¼ tsp pepper
6 medium bell peppers, any colour
1 cup shredded cheddar cheese

In a small saucepan over high heat, bring 1 cup water to a boil. Add a pinch of salt and the rice. Return to a boil, stir once, turn down the heat to low, cover, and simmer for 15 minutes. Turn off the heat and let sit, still covered, for 2 minutes. Fluff with a fork and set aside.

In a large skillet over medium heat, cook the ground beef and onions until the meat is no longer pink and the onions are soft, 5–7 minutes. Stir in the slightly cooled cooked rice, tomato soup, and seasonings.

Preheat the oven to 375°F.

Slice the tops off the peppers and carefully remove the seeds. Set the tops aside to use for another recipe (or to nibble on while this dish cooks).

Pour ¼ cup water into a 2½-quart casserole dish. Spoon the meat mixture into the peppers and place them in the casserole dish. Cover with aluminum foil or a lid and bake until the peppers are tender and the meat is hot and bubbly, about 40 minutes. Uncover and top with the shredded cheese. Bake for 5 more minutes. Set under the broiler for an additional 2 minutes if you like your cheese toasted.

Store leftovers in an airtight container in the refrigerator for up to 3 days. You can also freeze the filling in an airtight container for up to 3 months. Thaw overnight in the refrigerator before using.

Savoury Tomato Pie

Serves 6
25 minutes prep
2 hours total

A meatless dish that can be either a main or a side, this tomato pie is a southern U.S. classic. For the best flavour, make it in the summer when fresh field tomatoes are available. **Tamra**

---

3 field tomatoes
1 tsp salt, divided
1½ cups shredded old cheddar cheese
½ cup shredded mozzarella cheese
⅔ cup mayonnaise
1 clove garlic, crushed and minced
⅓ cup chopped green onions, whites included
10 basil leaves, roughly chopped
1 (9-inch) blind-baked pie crust (see page 179), ⅛ batch Homemade Pie Dough (page 171) or store-bought
Salt and pepper

Cut the tomatoes into ¼-inch slices. Lay them on a wire rack and season evenly with ½ tsp of the salt. Flip them over and salt the other side with the remaining ½ tsp. Set the wire rack over the sink or a bowl to let the tomatoes drain for about 30 minutes. Blot the tomatoes with a paper towel, then flip them and allow to sit for 30 more minutes before blotting the other side.

Preheat the oven to 350°F.

In a medium bowl, mix the cheeses with the mayonnaise. Set aside.

In a small bowl, toss together the garlic, green onions, and basil.

Line the bottom of the baked pie shell with half of the tomatoes (it's fine if they overlap). Sprinkle on half of the herb mixture, then season with salt and pepper. Repeat, reserving about 1 Tbsp of the herb mixture for a garnish.

Carefully spread the cheese and mayonnaise mixture over the tomato and herb layers. Sprinkle the reserved herb mixture in the middle of the top of the pie.

Bake until firm to the touch, 30–35 minutes. Let sit for 10 minutes before serving.

This is best eaten the day you make it. Leftovers do not store well.

Chapter 6

Desserts and Coffee Breaks

Precious Memories

Some of my earliest memories are of sitting on a tall stool in the corner of the packing shed (the building where we sort and pack our fruits and vegetables into boxes), watching Nana serve up her favourite seasonal desserts such as Plum Cake (page 185) or Apple Slice (page 173) at the morning coffee break. Grandpa, Dad, and Mom would pause their work just long enough to enjoy a cup of coffee and a sweet treat handmade by Nana. I didn't know it at the time, but these were not simple desserts to whip up! She must have spent hours organizing and preparing them, only to have us consume them in minutes before rushing back out the door. While these moments seemed brief and insignificant at the time, they are now sealed in my mind: moments of happiness, of togetherness, of hard work, family, and warmth. It was the people that made these moments so special, and now that I am grown, the recipes that were shared have become the symbol of these cherished moments.

This chapter is a collection of our family's favourite desserts and coffee break snacks that have been made again and again throughout the years. Some of them are simple, and some are more complex, but they each have a lifetime of memories attached to them. Like most of our recipes, the majority of them are made with produce that is grown on our farm. However, we have snuck in a few chocolate classics that we love to make in the winter when the fruit trees are taking a break—or whenever else we need a little dose of chocolate!

For me, tasting Nana's Apple Slice and Plum Cake will forever take me back to those happy moments shared with the family working together on the farm. As you try some of these seasonal treats, I'd encourage you to choose a few to bake on repeat. Make them your own by sharing them with your friends and family over and over again. Traditions don't have to be elaborate or fancy. They often start from a simple, happy moment together.

Laura

Homemade Pie Dough

Dough for 4 double-crust
or 8 single-crust pies
10 minutes prep
10 minutes total

I can't tell you how many times I watched my mom mix and roll pie dough. If we were lucky, we got to roll up our sleeves and help her push the rolling pin, forward and back, forward and back, creating a smooth surface like a sheet of ice. Mom's finger would fly round, tucking the perfectly rolled dough into the pie pan, heaping in the filling, sealing it shut, and fluting the edges. But the best moment of all came after supper, when large, warm slices were served piled high with dripping ice cream. I'm thankful for these idyllic childhood memories that stem from the outwardly most basic and mundane task of keeping the family fed. Be careful not to write off seemingly unimportant or commonplace moments. Sometimes they are the most precious of all. **Rachel**

- 5 cups all-purpose flour, plus more for kneading
- 2 tsp granulated sugar
- 1½ tsp salt
- 1 tsp baking powder
- 1 lb cold baking lard, cubed (I like Tenderflake)
- 1 egg
- 2 Tbsp vinegar
- ⅔ cup milk (approx.)

Note: This recipe makes a big batch for a few reasons. Because lard usually comes in 1 lb packages and 1 egg is difficult to reduce, it is easier to make a full batch than to try to split it. But that is to your benefit, because this dough keeps in the refrigerator for a whole week and freezes very nicely. I suggest freezing it in portion sizes because it cannot be refrozen.

In the bowl of a stand mixer fitted with a whisk attachment, combine the flour, sugar, salt, and baking powder. With the mixer running on low speed, drop the lard in several pieces at a time. Stop the mixer when the lard is all incorporated. Switch the attachment from a whisk to a dough hook.

Place the egg and vinegar in a glass measuring cup. Beat lightly with a fork. Add enough milk to bring the measurement up to 1 cup. Pour this over the lard mixture and mix until the dough forms a ball (add more flour if necessary). Knead in the mixer, or by hand, until the dough is just smooth and comes together into a ball, about 1 minute. Do not overmix!

Store in an airtight bag in the refrigerator for 1 week or in the freezer for up to 3 months.

Nana's Apple Slice

Serves 24
1 hour prep
2 hours total,
plus chilling and cooling

Grandpa still talks about how Nana's mom could make the most delicious pies. He even goes so far as to say that he married into the family to guarantee access to those pies! Well, Nana obviously inherited her mother's baking skills and has put them to good use. This recipe is Nana's signature dessert. It's more of a strudel than a traditional pie, though. It feeds a crowd, but it can easily be halved and baked in a quarter sheet pan if you prefer. If you halve the recipe, reduce the baking time to 35–45 minutes. **Laura**

Nana's Pastry Dough
3¾ cups all-purpose flour
1 tsp salt
1½ cups cold butter or margarine, cubed
1 cup milk
2 egg yolks

Filling
16 cups peeled, cored, and chopped apples (12–14 apples) (see note)
2 cups granulated sugar
¼ cup cornstarch
2 tsp ground cinnamon
2 egg whites
1 batch Vanilla Drizzle Icing (page 59)

Note: Golden Delicious, Mutsu, Spartan, and Honeycrisp are great choices of apples for this slice.

A FARM FAVOURITE

For the pastry dough
Stir together the flour and salt in a large mixing bowl. Using a pastry cutter, 2 forks, or a food processor fitted with the steel blade, cut in the butter until the butter pieces are no larger than a pea.

Measure out the milk in a glass measuring cup. Add both egg yolks and beat lightly with a fork (reserve the egg whites for egg-washing the slice). Pour the milk mixture over the flour in the bowl. Stir to create a stiff dough. Knead the dough just enough to form it into a ball. Wrap the dough in plastic wrap and let it chill in the refrigerator for at least 1 hour, and up to 5 days.

For the filling
Preheat the oven to 375°F. Have a 13 × 18-inch rimmed baking sheet nearby.

Place the apples in a large bowl.

In a separate bowl, stir together the sugar, cornstarch, and cinnamon. Set aside.

Cut the dough into 2 portions, making one slightly larger than the other. Roll the larger piece into a rectangle, about 15 × 20 inches (slightly larger than the baking sheet). Place the rolled dough into the baking sheet, gently tucking it into the corners without stretching it. Trim off any overhanging dough and add the scraps to the remaining piece of dough. Dump the apples into the crust, spreading them evenly and patting them down firmly. Sprinkle the cinnamon-sugar mixture evenly over the apples.

Roll out the second piece of dough into a slightly smaller rectangle, about 14 × 19 inches. Dip your finger in water and moisten the edge of the dough in the pan. »

» Immediately place the second piece of rolled dough on top of the apples. Trim any overhanging edges, and crimp shut with your fingers or a fork. Cut some vents in the centre of your slice (this is a good opportunity to show off some artistic flair!).

In a small bowl, whisk the egg whites until just bubbly. Using a pastry brush, brush this egg wash over the top of the pastry.

Bake until the top crust is golden brown and the apples are soft, 50–55 minutes.

Let the slice cool in the pan for at least 1 hour. Before serving, drizzle with the icing. Cut the slice into portions while it's still in the pan.

Leftovers can be covered loosely with plastic wrap and kept on the counter for up to 2 days.

Apple Hand-Pies

18 hand-pies
30 minutes prep
45 minutes total

A treat from my childhood, these little hand-pies are the cutest surprise to tuck into your kids' lunchboxes. A labour of love, nothing says "I love you" better than a fresh apple pie! I like to freeze any we don't eat right away and then pull them out as needed to ensure a flaky crust and fresh flavour. **Rachel**

- 3 cups peeled, cored, and finely diced apples (I like Mutsu, Honeycrisp, Spartan, or Arlet)
- ¼ cup granulated sugar
- ½ tsp ground cinnamon
- ⅛ tsp ground nutmeg
- Pinch of salt
- ¼ batch Homemade Pie Dough (page 171), or ½ bag Davison Farmhouse Pie Dough
- 1 batch Vanilla Drizzle Icing (page 59)

Preheat the oven to 425°F. Line a rimmed baking sheet with parchment paper.

In a large bowl, mix together the apples, sugar, cinnamon, nutmeg, and salt.

Roll out the dough to about ⅛ inch thick. Using a 5-inch round cookie cutter, cut the dough into 18 circles. You may need to re-roll the dough scraps to get 18 circles.

Working with 1 circle at a time, spoon about 2 Tbsp of apples onto the middle of each circle. Use a pastry brush to wet half the circle's edge with water. Fold the circle in half and seal the edges with a fork. Place on the prepared baking sheet and repeat with the remaining filling and dough. Poke some venting holes with a fork in the top of each hand-pie.

Bake until the apples are soft and bubbly and the crust is golden brown, about 15 minutes. Transfer to a wire rack to cool completely before drizzling with the icing.

Store leftovers in a loosely covered container on the counter for up to 2 days or in the freezer for up to 4 months.

Fresh Raspberry Pie

Serves 6–8
1 hour prep
3 hours total

This pie is every bit as decadent as it looks. Mountains of fresh raspberries held together by a luscious glaze, with a hint of cream cheese to balance it all out, make this dessert an absolute showstopper. **Laura**

- ⅓ cup spreadable cream cheese
- 1 Tbsp icing sugar
- 1 tsp vanilla extract
- 1½ cups granulated sugar
- ⅓ cup cornstarch
- 5–6 cups raspberries, divided (about 4 pints)
- 2 cups water, divided
- 1 Tbsp lemon juice
- 1 (9-inch) blind-baked pie crust (see below), Homemade Pie Dough (page 171) or store-bought
- 3 fresh mint leaves, for garnish (optional)
- Whipped cream for serving (optional)

In a stand mixer fitted with the paddle attachment, beat the cream cheese, icing sugar, and vanilla on medium to high speed until smooth, about 5 minutes. Set aside.

In a small bowl, stir together the sugar and cornstarch. Set aside.

Place 1 cup of the raspberries and 1 cup of the water in a medium saucepan. Stirring frequently, bring to a boil over medium heat and simmer, uncovered, for 3 minutes. Place a fine mesh strainer over a bowl and carefully pour the cooked raspberries through to strain out the seeds. Discard the seeds and return the juice to the pot. Add the remaining 1 cup of water and whisk in the sugar and cornstarch mixture. Return to a boil over medium heat and simmer, stirring constantly, until the glaze is thick and translucent, about 2 minutes. Stir in the lemon juice.

Spread the cream cheese mixture evenly over the bottom of the baked pie crust. Arrange ⅓ of the remaining fresh raspberries over the cream cheese. Pour ⅓ of the glaze over the raspberries. Repeat twice. Garnish with fresh mint leaves (if using).

Refrigerate, uncovered, for at least 2 hours and up to 8 hours before serving. Serve with lightly sweetened whipped cream (if using).

Cover leftovers with plastic wrap and store in the refrigerator for up to 3 days.

Blind-Baking a Pie Crust

Many pies, such as fresh fruit or cream pies, call for a blind-baked pie shell. That just means you bake the crust before you add your filling. This can be tricky, as the dough shrinks while baking. Follow these directions for success:

Preheat the oven to 350°F.

Roll out your pie dough to about ⅛ inch thick and about 12 inches in diameter. Fit the pastry into an ungreased pie plate. Trim and crimp the edges as desired. Gently place a piece of aluminum foil, shiny side down, on the pie shell. Fill with pie weights, dried beans or rice.

Bake until the edges are starting to brown, 15–20 minutes. Remove the foil and weights. Using a fork, prick the edges and bottom of the shell to keep air bubbles from forming. Return to the oven until the shell is golden brown, 6–9 minutes.

Pear Cardamom Crisp

Serves 6
35 minutes prep
1 hour, 20 minutes total

Fresh, juicy pears spiked with cinnamon and cardamom make this simple dessert a delight for the senses. This gem of a recipe was created by my sister-in-law Leah, who grew up playing under the pear trees at Davison Orchards. The catalyst was her recent love affair with cardamom. Take my word for it: it's worthy of a spot at your table! **Rachel**

Davison's Crumble Topping

- 1 cup quick oats
- ¾ cup all-purpose flour
- ⅔ cup brown sugar, lightly packed
- ½ tsp baking soda
- ¼ tsp salt
- ½ cup cold butter or margarine, cubed

Pear Cardamom Crisp

- 1½ Tbsp all-purpose flour
- 1 Tbsp granulated sugar
- 1 tsp ground cinnamon
- ½ tsp ground cardamom
- 6 pears, peeled, cored, and chopped
- 1½ cups Davison's Crumble Topping

Vanilla ice cream, for serving

For the crumble topping

In a large bowl, mix together the oats, flour, sugar, baking soda, and salt.

Using a pastry blender, a fork, or your hands, cut in the butter until the mixture resembles coarse crumbs. The butter pieces should be no larger than a pea.

Use right away or store in an airtight container in the refrigerator for up to 3 days or in the freezer for up to 3 months. You can use it straight from frozen.

For the crisp

Preheat the oven to 350°F. Lightly grease an 8 × 8-inch baking dish.

In a small bowl, stir together the flour, sugar, cinnamon, and cardamom. Add the pears and toss well in the flour mixture to coat.

Place the pears in the prepared baking dish and sprinkle the crumble over the top.

Set the dish on top of a rimmed baking dish to catch any juices that spill out while the crisp bakes.

Bake until the pears are bubbling and soft and the crumble topping is golden brown, 40–45 minutes.

Serve warm with a scoop of vanilla ice cream.

Store leftovers in an airtight container in the refrigerator for up to 3 days.

Pumpkin Cake

Serves 20
40 minutes prep
1 hour total,
plus cooling

One of the oldest recipes from the Davison Farmhouse Bakery, this sheet cake is still one of our customer favourites. Topped with maple cream cheese icing, this well-spiced and incredibly moist cake is the ideal autumn treat. This is a large sheet cake recipe, but leftovers freeze very well. **Laura**

Pumpkin Cake

2 cups pumpkin purée (see note on page 27)
1½ cups granulated sugar
1 cup canola or vegetable oil
4 eggs, lightly beaten
1 tsp vanilla extract
2 cups all-purpose flour
2 tsp baking soda
1½ tsp pumpkin pie spice
1 tsp ground cinnamon
1 tsp salt

Maple Cream Cheese Icing

½ package (4 oz/125 g) cream cheese, softened
3 Tbsp butter, softened
1 Tbsp half-and-half cream
1 tsp maple extract
2 cups icing sugar

Note: For a traditional cream cheese icing, replace the maple extract with the same quantity of vanilla extract.

For the cake

Preheat the oven to 350°F. Coat a 10 × 15 × 1-inch baking sheet with cooking spray.

Beat the pumpkin purée, sugar, and oil together until well combined. Add the eggs and vanilla and beat well to combine.

In a separate bowl, whisk together the flour, baking soda, pumpkin pie spice, cinnamon, and salt. Add the dry ingredients to the pumpkin mixture and stir until well combined.

Pour into the prepared baking sheet and spread evenly. Bake until a toothpick inserted into the centre of the cake comes out clean, 25–30 minutes. Place on a wire rack to cool completely.

For the icing

Beat the cream cheese with the butter until light and fluffy.

Add the cream and maple extract and mix until well combined.

Slowly mix in the icing sugar, ½ cup at a time. Beat until the icing is smooth and airy, 2–3 minutes.

At this point, the icing can be stored in an airtight container in the refrigerator for up to 3 days or in the freezer for up to 2 months. Bring to room temperature and beat until fluffy before using.

Cover the cooled cake with the icing.

Leftover cake can be stored in an airtight container in the refrigerator for up to 3 days or in the freezer for up to 3 months.

A FARM FAVOURITE

Nana's Plum Cake

Serves 12
45 minutes prep
1½ hours total, plus cooling

Nana made this cake for years and years in the Davison Farmhouse Bakery. She was always very particular about how it was done: "The cake mustn't be too thick. The fruit needs to be placed so that it touches together on top of the batter. Don't be cheap with the crumble!" It is now a staple in my own home. Don't be nervous when you see how thin the batter is when you pour it in the pan. Remember, this is exactly how Nana does it and it makes for an extremely moist cake. Let the fruit be the star! **Laura**

Topping

- ½ cup brown sugar, lightly packed
- ¼ cup butter or margarine
- 1 tsp ground cinnamon

Cake

- 1 cup granulated sugar
- ¼ cup butter or margarine
- 2 eggs
- 1 tsp vanilla extract
- 1½ cups all-purpose flour
- 1 tsp baking powder
- ½ tsp salt
- ½ cup milk
- 5 cups halved and pitted Italian prune plums (see note)
- 1 batch Vanilla Drizzle Icing (page 59)

Note: You can use apricots or peaches in place of the plums, and it works just as well with frozen fruit as it does fresh. If you decide to use frozen fruit, allow the fruit to partially thaw before using and increase the baking time by about 15 minutes.

Preheat the oven to 350°F. Thoroughly grease a 9 × 13-inch baking dish.

For the topping

In a small bowl, mix together the sugar, butter, and cinnamon, using your fingers to make a crumble. Set aside.

For the cake

Using a stand mixer fitted with the paddle attachment, cream the sugar and butter together on medium speed. Beat in the eggs and vanilla until smooth. In a separate bowl, stir together the flour, baking powder, and salt.

With the mixer running on low speed, add the dry ingredients and milk alternately to the egg mixture, starting and ending with the dry ingredients. Do not overmix. Pour the batter into the prepared baking dish.

Arrange the plums on top of the cake batter so they are touching but not overlapping. The whole cake should be covered in fruit. Sprinkle the topping over the fruit.

Bake until the middle of the cake bounces back when pressed lightly, 30–40 minutes. Let cool completely before drizzling with the icing.

Leftovers can be stored in an airtight container on the counter for up to 3 days.

Rhubarb Cake

Serves 12
15 minutes prep
1 hour total

One of my most prized possessions is a stack of cookbooks that belonged to my grandma Eva. Not one of them is still bound—the pages are stained, tattered, and even ripped—but these flaws just make them all the more precious to me. Jotted down in the margins or tucked between the pages are my grandma's notes about adjustments she made, whether the recipe was a success or not, and life advice. These well-used cookbooks translated into skilfully prepared food, which in turn brought the family together to eat, laugh, and make memories. I hope this recipe brings your family together as it does mine. **Rachel**

Topping

1 cup granulated sugar
¼ cup all-purpose flour
½ tsp ground cinnamon
¼ cup butter or margarine

Cake

2 eggs, lightly beaten
1 cup granulated sugar
1 cup heavy cream that's gone sour (see note)
1 tsp vanilla extract
2 cups all-purpose flour
1 tsp baking soda
½ tsp salt
2½ cups chopped fresh or frozen rhubarb

Note: You want your heavy cream to be just a couple of days past the expiry date. It should smell pleasantly sour, not rancid. If you don't have expired cream, you can substitute 1 cup fresh heavy cream mixed with 1 tsp vinegar.

Preheat the oven to 350°F. Lightly coat a 9 × 13-inch baking dish with cooking spray.

For the topping
In a small bowl, mix together the sugar, flour, and cinnamon. Add the butter and use your fingers to mix it in to make a crumble. Set aside.

For the cake
In a large bowl, mix together the eggs and sugar. Stir in the cream and vanilla. Add the flour, baking soda, and salt and mix well. Fold in the rhubarb. Spread the mixture into the prepared baking pan. Sprinkle the topping over the cake.

Bake until a toothpick inserted in the centre of the cake comes out clean, 40–45 minutes.

Store in an airtight container on the counter for up to 2 days or freeze for up to 3 months.

"Daddy Is Great" Chocolate Cake

Serves 12
25 minutes prep
1 hour total, plus cooling

My dad has never made a chocolate cake in his life, and yet he has always gotten all the credit for this one. Every time Mom baked this cake we would pound the table and chant: "Daddy is great, he makes us chocolate cake!" I can picture Mom in the background, arms crossed, smirking and shaking her head. Dad would cut us huge pieces and we would all indulge like it was Christmas. Truth is, we didn't care who made it, as long as we got a big piece! **Laura**

Chocolate Cake

- 3 cups all-purpose flour
- 2 cups granulated sugar
- 6 Tbsp cocoa powder
- 2 tsp baking soda
- 1 tsp salt
- 2 cups water
- ⅔ cup canola oil
- 2 Tbsp white vinegar
- 1 Tbsp vanilla extract

Icing

- 2 cups icing sugar
- 3 Tbsp cocoa powder
- 3 Tbsp butter, softened
- 1½ tsp pure vanilla extract
- ¼ cup warm water (approx. 115°F, see note)

Note: The water should be hot from the tap but not boiling, otherwise the icing will separate. The ideal cooling period for the cake is 2 hours before topping with icing. Learn from my mistake: don't attempt to ice it right out of the oven! The icing will separate and slide right off!

For the cake

Preheat the oven to 350°F. Grease a 9 × 13-inch baking dish with butter or margarine.

In a large bowl, whisk together the flour, sugar, cocoa powder, baking soda, and salt. Add the water, oil, vinegar, and vanilla. Beat until smooth, about 2 minutes.

Pour the batter into the prepared pan and bake until a toothpick inserted in the centre comes out clean, about 35 minutes. Allow the cake to cool in the pan for about 2 hours before icing.

When the cake is cool, make the icing.

For the icing

Using a stand mixer fitted with a paddle attachment, mix together the icing sugar, cocoa powder, butter, and vanilla on low speed.

With the mixer still running on low speed, slowly add the warm water, mixing until everything is combined. Increase the speed to medium for about 1 minute and then increase it to high speed. Beat on high until the icing is light and fluffy, about 3 minutes.

This icing hardens in about 15 minutes, so make it right before you plan to ice your cake.

Cover the cake with the icing and serve straight from the pan.

Store leftovers in an airtight container on the counter for up to 3 days, or freeze the cake, uniced, for up to 1 month.

No-Bake Cheesecake with Fruit Compote

Serves 9
45 minutes prep
45 minutes total, plus chilling

This simple no-bake cheesecake was served at my parents' wedding many years ago. Lighter than a traditional cheesecake, it is a nice way to finish off a celebratory meal. The base freezes well, and the fruit compote can be made a day ahead of time, leaving no prep to do on the day you plan to serve it. **Rachel**

Crust

- 1½ cups graham cracker crumbs, plus more for garnish
- ⅓ cup icing sugar
- ⅓ cup melted butter or margarine

Cream Cheese Filling

- 1 (8 oz/250 g) package cream cheese, at room temperature
- ½ cup icing sugar
- 2 cups freshly whipped cream
- Dash vanilla extract

Fruit Compote

- 2 cups chopped fresh or thawed from frozen fruit (pitted sweet cherries, blueberries, apricots, and peaches all work well)
- ¼ cup granulated sugar
- ¼ cup water
- 2 tsp cornstarch
- ½ tsp vanilla extract

For the crust
Stir together the graham crumbs, icing sugar, and butter until fully combined. Press firmly into an ungreased 9 × 9-inch cake pan.

For the filling
In the bowl of a stand mixer fitted with the whisk attachment, beat the cream cheese and icing sugar on high speed until light and fluffy. Using a spatula, fold in the whipped cream until incorporated. Stir in the vanilla. Drop the filling by spoonfuls onto the graham cracker crust and spread until smooth. Cover with plastic wrap and chill for at least 1½ hours, or up to 2 days.

For the fruit compote
Meanwhile, place the fruit, sugar, and water in a medium saucepan. Bring to a boil over medium heat, then turn down the heat to low and simmer, stirring often, until the fruit is very soft, 10–15 minutes.

In a small bowl, mix the cornstarch with 1 Tbsp cold water to make it pourable. Slowly add to the softened fruit, stirring, until the desired consistency has been reached. Let cook, stirring constantly, for 1 minute, just to finish the thickening process. Remove from the heat and stir in the vanilla. Refrigerate until chilled, at least 1½ hours, or up to 2 days.

When you are ready to serve, spread the fruit compote over the cheesecake. Cut into slices and serve.

Store leftovers in an airtight container in the refrigerator for up to 2 days.

Vanilla-Pear Cheesecake Bars

8–12 bars
30 minutes prep
1 hour total,
plus 3 hours for chilling

If you are looking for a special dessert to bring to an event, may I suggest this one? With their pecan crust, cream cheese centre, and pear topping, I am confident that these bars will quickly become a household favourite. This recipe comes from my sister Leah, and it always reminds me of her hospitality. **Laura**

- ¾ cup all-purpose flour
- ½ cup quick oats
- ½ cup finely chopped pecans, plus 2 Tbsp broken into large pieces, divided
- ¾ cup sugar plus 1 tsp, divided
- ½ cup melted butter
- 1 (8 oz/250g) package cream cheese, at room temperature
- 1 egg
- 1 tsp vanilla extract
- 3 ripe pears (Bosc or Bartlett is ideal)
- ½ tsp ground cinnamon
- Freshly whipped cream for serving (optional)

Preheat the oven to 350°F. Lightly grease a 9 × 9-inch baking dish.

In a large bowl, stir together the flour, oats, ½ cup finely chopped pecans, and ¼ cup of the sugar. Stir in the melted butter until well combined. Press the mixture firmly into the bottom of the prepared baking pan. Bake the crust for 10 minutes and set aside to cool slightly. Leave the oven on.

In the bowl of a stand mixer fitted with the whisk attachment, beat ½ cup of the sugar, the cream cheese, egg, and vanilla until smooth. Pour over the crust.

Peel the pears and cut them into quarters, discarding the core. Carefully arrange the pear quarters on the cream cheese layer, close but not overlapping and reaching all the way to the edge of the pan. The pears will sink down, which is perfect.

Combine the remaining 1 tsp sugar with the cinnamon. Sprinkle this over the pears. Top with the 2 Tbsp of broken pecan pieces.

Bake until well set around the edges, about 30 minutes. Remove from the oven. The centre will be soft, but it will set as it cools. Place on a wire rack on the counter to cool in the pan for 1 hour, then cover with plastic wrap and refrigerate for at least 2 hours, or up to 3 days.

Cut into bars and serve with a dollop of whipped cream (if using).

Store leftovers in an airtight container in the refrigerator for up to 3 days.

Strawberry Shortcake

12 shortcakes
20 minutes prep
35 minutes total, plus chilling

This is another of Nana's recipes. It's a springtime staple in all of our homes. Fresh biscuits, sun-ripened strawberries, and sweet whipped cream? Yes, please! **Tamra**

Biscuits

- 2 cups all-purpose flour
- ¼ cup granulated sugar
- 4 tsp baking powder
- ¾ tsp salt
- ¼ cup cold butter or margarine
- ¾ cup milk

Filling

- 3 cups sliced strawberries
- 2 Tbsp granulated sugar

Whipped Cream

- 2 cups heavy cream
- ¼ cup icing sugar
- 2 tsp vanilla extract

Preheat the oven to 400°F. Line a baking sheet with parchment paper.

For the biscuits

In a large bowl, whisk together the flour, sugar, baking powder, and salt. Using a pastry blender, a fork, or your hands, cut in the butter until the mixture resembles coarse crumbs. The butter pieces should be no larger than a pea. Alternatively, pulse the dry ingredients and the butter in a food processor fitted with the steel blade. Pour the milk over the dry mixture and stir to make a soft dough.

Turn the dough out onto a lightly floured surface and knead gently 6–8 times, just enough to bring it together into a ball.

Using your hands, pat the dough to about ½ inch thick. Using a 2½-inch round cookie cutter, cut out 12 biscuits. Place the biscuits on the prepared baking pan, close together for soft-sided biscuits or 1 inch apart for crusty ones.

Bake until lightly browned on top, 13–15 minutes.

For the filling

While the biscuits are baking, toss the sliced strawberries with the sugar. Let stand for at least 5 minutes. The sugar will pull the juices out of the strawberries to make a nice filling.

For the whipped cream

In the bowl of a stand mixer fitted with a whisk attachment, whip the cream on medium-high speed until frothy and starting to thicken. Add the sugar and vanilla and continue to whip until soft peaks form. Cover the bowl with plastic wrap and refrigerate until ready to serve, up to 4 hours.

To assemble the shortcakes

Slice the biscuits in half and fill them with the strawberries, sandwich-style. Top with a generous helping of whipped cream and more strawberries. Serve immediately. These do not store well once filled.

Chocolate Sundae Pudding

Serves 6–8
15 minutes prep
55 minutes total

As a teenager, this dessert was my way of telling my dad that I loved him. Sometimes it is hard to speak your thoughts, so I would bake mine. This old-fashioned pudding is his favourite treat, and it is a symbol of love and respect between us. I still think of him every time I make it, whether he will be eating with us or not. **Rachel**

Sauce
1⅔ cups water
¾ cup granulated sugar
2 Tbsp butter or margarine
1 Tbsp cocoa powder
½ tsp salt

Cake
1 cup all-purpose flour
⅔ cup granulated sugar
2 Tbsp cocoa powder
2 tsp baking powder
¼ tsp salt
3 Tbsp butter or margarine
1 egg
⅔ cup milk

Vanilla ice cream, for serving

Preheat the oven to 350°F. Lightly grease an 8 × 8-inch glass baking dish.

For the sauce
In a small saucepan over medium heat, combine the water with the sugar, butter, cocoa powder, and salt. Heat, stirring occasionally, until the butter is melted and the mixture is steaming hot.

For the cake
In a mixing bowl, whisk together the flour, sugar, cocoa powder, baking powder, and salt. Using 2 forks or your hands, cut in the butter until it resembles fine crumbs. The butter pieces should be no larger than a pea. In a glass measuring cup, lightly beat the egg and milk. Pour this over the flour mixture and stir to just combine.

Carefully pour the hot sauce into the prepared baking dish. Drop the cake batter onto the sauce by spoonfuls, making 6–8 dumplings.

Bake until a toothpick inserted in the centre comes out clean, about 40 minutes. Let stand for 15 minutes before serving warm. Scoop 1 cake dumpling into a bowl and top with vanilla ice cream. Pour a generous scoop of the sauce over the ice cream. Serve immediately.

This is best eaten the day it's made but leftovers can be covered with plastic wrap and stored on the counter for 1 day.

Chapter 7

Cookies, Sweets, and Treats

DAVISON
ORCHARDS

Procrasti-Baking

There are certain tasks that I do because they are necessary to live a healthy, responsible life. Then there are the tasks that I do more because I want to than because I have to, as a hobby rather than out of necessity. For me, cooking falls into the first category. It is my responsibility to organize and prepare three meals a day for my family. Don't misunderstand me, I enjoy cooking! There are few things that are more satisfying than taking the time to prepare a meal and having the pleasure of watching your family wolf it down, leaving the dishes scraped clean. No leftovers signifies a job well done. But then there is baking. While I would love to put this pastime of mine into the mandatory category, I'll be honest in saying that most of the things I bake we could live without. Technically, anyway.

There is a phenomenon that occurs regularly in my household. I'll be organizing my time or trying to figure out what to cook for supper when all of a sudden I'm in the kitchen, apron on, baking! Making cookies wasn't on the agenda, but here I am, spoon in hand. Furthermore, there comes with this unplanned baking a peculiar urgency that seems to come out of nowhere. All I know is that the flour is flying, the chocolate chips are out, and I'm frantically whipping something up. Upon further thought, I am likely avoiding something: something stressful, or confrontational, or some chore that I hate doing. Then it dawns on me that, oh dear, I'm doing it again. I am procrasti-baking!

This chapter is chock full of our favourite procrasti-baking recipes. Many of them were originally Rachel's cookie recipes that we have since adopted as our own. Most of them are pretty quick to whip up and can be made with little to no planning, as they call for everyday pantry ingredients.

If you are also a procrasti-baker, I hope you enjoy these recipes as much as I do. Go ahead and bake them, avoiding that looming task for just a few minutes more.

Laura

DAVISON
ORCHARDS
COUNTRY VILLAGE
Pyrex
ARTISAN

Pumpkin Spice Snickerdoodles

42 cookies or
21 sandwiches
20 minutes prep
1 hour, 10 minutes total

These cookies boast a slight twist on traditional snickerdoodles and are the perfect nod to autumn. A fun way to eat them is as an ice-cream sandwich: the ideal treat for a sunny day. **Laura**

Cookie Dough

1 cup butter or margarine
1 cup granulated sugar
½ cup brown sugar, lightly packed
2 egg yolks
½ cup pumpkin purée (see note on page 27)
3 cups all-purpose flour
2 tsp cream of tartar
1 tsp baking soda
2 tsp pumpkin pie spice
1 tsp ground cinnamon
½ tsp salt

Cinnamon Sugar

⅓ cup granulated sugar
1½ tsp ground cinnamon

Vanilla ice cream for serving (optional)

Note: We think cookies are best eaten fresh! While this is a contentious point with our families, we don't believe cookies should be stored on the counter. We recommend that you enjoy some fresh the day they are baked and then store the rest in an airtight container in the freezer for up to 3 months. When you are ready for cookies, simply pull them out of the freezer, let them thaw for 10–20 minutes on the counter, and then enjoy.

For the cookie dough
In a large bowl, cream together the butter and both sugars until light and fluffy. Add the egg yolks and beat until creamy. Add the pumpkin purée and mix well.

In a separate bowl, whisk together the flour, cream of tartar, baking soda, spices, and salt. Fold the flour mixture into the pumpkin mixture, until well combined.

Cover with plastic wrap and refrigerate the dough for at least ½ hour.

For the cinnamon sugar
In a small bowl, mix together the sugar and cinnamon using your hands or a small spoon.

To bake the cookies
Preheat the oven to 350°F. Line 2 baking sheets with parchment paper (you will need to bake the cookies in batches).

Roll the cookie dough into 1¼-inch balls, then dip each ball into the cinnamon sugar, swirling to coat completely. Place on the prepared baking sheet, 12 cookies per pan, leaving enough space to allow the cookies to spread. Press the cookies down lightly with the bottom of a glass or the palm of your hand.

Bake in the centre of the oven until lightly golden, 10–12 minutes. Let the cookies cool on the pan for 5 minutes before transferring them to a wire cooling rack to cool completely.

Repeat until all the cookies are baked. If desired, sandwich a generous scoop of vanilla ice cream between 2 cookies. Enjoy immediately.

Classic Chocolate Chip Cookies

36 cookies
15 minutes prep
50 minutes total

When I was a child, my cousin would often bring these cookies to school in his lunch. Since my mom was adamant that chocolate chip cookies must always be full of oatmeal, I was seriously jealous. Occasionally he would have mercy on me and let me have a bite of a cookie. As soon as I was old enough to bake independently, I phoned my aunt and begged her for the recipe. Ironically, now I am the mom baking oatmeal chocolate chip cookies. But once in a while I remember my childhood plight and I bake up a large batch of these to appease my children and husband. **Rachel**

- 1 cup butter or margarine
- ¾ cup granulated sugar
- ½ cup brown sugar, lightly packed
- 2 eggs
- 1½ tsp vanilla extract
- 2½ cups all-purpose flour
- 1 tsp baking soda
- ½ tsp salt
- 1½ cups semisweet chocolate chips

Preheat the oven to 350°F. Line 2 baking sheets with parchment paper (you will need to bake the cookies in batches).

In a large bowl, cream together the butter and both sugars. Add the eggs one at a time, beating well after each addition. Stir in the vanilla.

In a separate bowl, stir together the flour, baking soda, and salt. Fold the flour mixture into the butter and egg mixture, until well combined. Do not overmix. Fold in the chocolate chips.

Using a dessert spoon, drop the cookie dough onto the prepared baking sheets, 12 cookies per pan. Allow each cookie some space to spread.

Bake the cookies, one pan at a time, until lightly golden brown around the edges, 10–12 minutes. Do not overbake. Let the cookies cool on the pan for 5 minutes before transferring them to a wire cooling rack to cool completely.

Repeat until all the cookies are baked. See note on page 205 for storage tips.

Peanut Butter Flax Cookies

72 cookies
15 minutes prep
1 hour, 20 minutes total

This is my grandma's signature cookie recipe. Every single time I visit her, she serves these cookies alongside a pitcher of Five Alive. There is comfort in the predictable. I often make these cookies for my family and friends. My favourite thing about them (aside from the fact that they are completely addictive and delicious) is that they are flourless, making them a great treat for people who can't eat gluten. **Rachel**

- 1 cup brown sugar, lightly packed
- ¾ cup granulated sugar
- 1½ cups peanut butter, smooth or crunchy
- ½ cup butter or margarine
- 3 eggs, lightly beaten
- 1 tsp vanilla extract
- 4 cups quick oats
- ⅓ cup freshly ground flax seed
- 2 tsp baking soda
- ½ tsp salt
- ½ cup semisweet chocolate chips
- ½ cup dried cranberries

Preheat the oven to 350°F. Line 2 baking sheets with parchment paper (you will need to bake the cookies in batches).

In a large bowl, cream both sugars with the peanut butter and butter. Add the eggs one at a time, beating well after each addition. Stir in the vanilla.

Add the oats, ground flax seed, baking soda, and salt to the bowl. Fold to incorporate. Fold in the chocolate chips and dried cranberries.

Using a dessert spoon, drop the cookie dough onto the prepared baking sheets, 12 cookies per pan. Allow each cookie some space to spread.

Bake the cookies, one pan at a time, until browned around the edges and dry on top, 10–11 minutes. Let cool for 5 minutes on the pan before transferring to a wire rack.

Repeat until all the cookies are baked. See note on page 205 for storage tips.

Davison Ginger Chews

16 large cookies
20 minutes prep
45 minutes total

Here it is: the recipe for our farm's best-selling cookie! With show-stopping visual appeal, this cookie is easy to make, is irresistibly chewy and soft on the inside but slightly crisp on the outside, and even boasts a long shelf life. What's not to love? **Tamra**

¾ cup butter or margarine
1 cup granulated sugar
1 egg
½ cup fancy molasses
2½ cups all-purpose flour
2 tsp baking soda
2 tsp ground ginger
1 tsp ground cinnamon
½ tsp salt
½ cup coarse sugar, for rolling (see note)

Notes: If you don't want jumbo-sized cookies, you can divide the dough into 32 pieces and reduce the baking time to 10–11 minutes.

You can use regular sugar for rolling the cookies if you don't have coarse sugar.

This cookie dough freezes well. Thaw completely in the refrigerator overnight before using and then bake as directed.

Preheat the oven to 350°F. Line 2 baking sheets with parchment paper (you will need to bake the cookies in batches).

In a large bowl, cream together the butter and sugar. Add the egg and molasses and beat well.

In a separate bowl, stir together the flour, baking soda, spices, and salt. Fold the flour mixture into the butter and egg mixture, until well combined. Divide the dough into 16 evenly sized pieces. Shape each piece into a ball and roll it in the coarse sugar to cover completely.

Allowing a generous amount of space for the cookies to spread, place 8 balls of dough on each baking sheet, and press lightly with the bottom of a glass or the palm of your hand.

Bake the cookies one pan at a time until slightly cracked on top, about 12 minutes. Remove from the oven and bang the bottom of the cookie sheet lightly on the counter. This will help make beautiful cracks on your ginger chew. Let cool on the pan for 1 minute before transferring to a wire rack to cool completely. Repeat with the other pan.

Because of the molasses in these cookies, they don't dry out quickly and, for a cookie, have a great shelf life. These can be kept in an airtight container on your counter for up to 4 days or in the freezer for up to 4 months.

A FARM FAVOURITE

Chocolate Chip Oatmeal Cookies

48 cookies
15 minutes prep
1 hour, 10 minutes total

If I could make only one kind of cookie for the rest of my life, I would choose these. With their soft and chewy centres and slight crunch around the edges, they boast every attribute that makes up a good cookie. I can even convince myself that they make a healthy snack thanks to all that oatmeal! **Rachel**

---

1 cup butter or margarine
1 cup brown sugar, lightly packed
¾ cup granulated sugar
2 eggs
1 tsp vanilla extract
1¾ cups all-purpose flour
1 tsp baking soda
½ tsp salt
2½ cups quick oats
1½ cups semisweet chocolate chips

Preheat the oven to 350°F. Line 2 baking sheets with parchment paper (you will need to bake the cookies in batches).

In a large bowl, cream together the butter and both sugars. Add the eggs one at a time, beating well after each addition. Stir in the vanilla.

In a small bowl, whisk together the flour, baking soda, and salt. Add to the butter mixture and stir well. Fold in the oats and chocolate chips.

Using a dessert spoon, drop the cookie dough onto the prepared baking sheets, 12 cookies per pan. Allow each cookie some space to spread.

Bake one pan at a time until the cookies are browned around the edges and dry on top, 11–14 minutes. Let cool for 5 minutes on the pan before transferring to a wire rack to cool completely.

Repeat until all the cookies are baked. See note on page 205 for storage tips.

Cheesecake Stuffed Strawberries

About 45 strawberries
20 minutes prep
20 minutes total

Last time I brought these to a potluck they almost caused a riot! They're just that good. **Rachel**

- 1 (8 oz/250 g) package cream cheese, at room temperature
- ¾ cup icing sugar
- 1 tsp vanilla extract
- 2–3 pints large, fresh strawberries
- Chocolate sauce, for serving (optional)

Place the cream cheese, icing sugar, and vanilla in the bowl of a stand mixer fitted with the whisk attachment. Beat on medium-high speed until smooth.

Remove the stems and cores of the strawberries with a paring knife. Slice off a small part of the tip so the strawberries can stand upright.

Fill a piping bag or a thick plastic bag with the cream cheese mixture. Snip off the corner of the bag and pipe the mixture into the strawberries. Fill the strawberries right to the top.

Serve right away or refrigerate for up to 2 hours until ready to serve. Before serving, drizzle with chocolate sauce (if using).

Leftovers don't store well, so eat them all up.

Apple Nachos

Serves about 6
10 minutes prep
10 minutes total

This is more of an idea than a recipe, and it's a good one. My sister Leah came up with this and has served it to many happy guests over the years. I suggest using Honeycrisp, Ambrosia, or Arlet apples as they are great for fresh eating and do not brown quickly once sliced. You can get creative with the toppings to make these your own. The sky's the limit! **Laura**

- 3 fresh apples, skin on
- ¼ cup Davison Old-Fashioned Caramel (see note)
- ¼ cup chopped pecans
- 2 Tbsp semisweet mini chocolate chips

Note: If Davison Old-Fashioned Caramel is unavailable, you can use about 5 oz of soft caramels. Unwrap the caramels and place them in a microwave-safe dish. Add 1 Tbsp of half-and-half cream. Microwave on high for 1 minute. Stir and microwave for 30 more seconds, or until smooth.

Core and thinly slice the apples, and arrange them on a serving platter.

Warm the caramel in the microwave for 15 seconds. If it is still too thick to run off a spoon, microwave for 10 more seconds or until pourable. Drizzle the warm caramel over the apple slices.

Top with the chopped pecans and chocolate chips. Serve immediately.

Caramel Apple Popcorn Balls

12 popcorn balls
20 minutes prep
20 minutes total

There is something so fun and old-fashioned about popcorn balls. These ones are especially easy to make because they use pre-made caramel. The dried apples add a nice, tangy surprise! Wrap individual balls in a cellophane bag tied with a ribbon for a fun Thanksgiving table favour. **Rachel**

½ cup popcorn kernels
1 (300 g) jar Davison Old-Fashioned Caramel (see note)
1 cup dehydrated apple chips, chopped (page 221)

Note: If Davison Old-Fashioned Caramel is unavailable, you can use about 10 oz of soft caramels. Unwrap the caramels and place them in a microwave-safe dish. Add 2 Tbsp of half-and-half cream. Microwave on high for 1½ minutes. Stir and microwave for 30 more seconds, or until smooth.

Pop the popcorn kernels using your preferred method. Dump the popped popcorn into a very large bowl. Line a baking sheet or tray with waxed paper.

Remove the lid of the caramel jar and place the jar in the microwave. Warm up the caramel in the microwave until it is pourable, about 25 seconds. Stir until smooth.

Add the apple chips to the popcorn. Pour over the warm caramel, stirring until the popcorn is evenly coated.

Dampen your hands with cold water. Taking a large handful, form the popcorn mixture into balls. Re-wet your hands when the caramel starts to stick to you.

Place the popcorn balls on the prepared tray and allow to set on the counter or in the refrigerator for 1 hour before serving.

These can be made up to 2 days in advance and stored in an airtight container in the refrigerator. You can also store them in an airtight container in the freezer for up to 1 month.

Oven-Dehydrated Apple Chips

1 cup dried apples
15 minutes prep
2 hours, 15 minutes total

My favourite apple for drying is Jonagold. No other apple can beat it for flavour when it comes to dehydrating! Honeycrisp, Mutsu, and McIntosh dry very nicely as well, though. **Rachel**

---

2 large fresh apples

Preheat the oven to 225°F. Line a rimmed baking sheet with parchment paper.

Peel the apples if desired. Core and thinly slice them into even slices, about ⅛ inch thick. Lay the slices on the prepared baking sheet. Do not let the slices touch.

Bake for 1 hour. Flip the slices and bake for another hour, or until the apples are dry to the touch.

Dried apples can be stored in an airtight container in a cool, dry place for up to 1 year.

Grilled Apricots

Serves 4
10 minutes prep
18 minutes total

A quick, early summer dessert, grilled apricots are a lovely way to enjoy a beautiful evening on the patio. Grilling fruit pulls out its natural sweetness. Peaches are equally delicious grilled, and if you don't love the taste of browned butter, use melted butter instead. **Rachel**

- 1 Tbsp butter
- 4 firm-ripe apricots
- Vanilla ice cream, for serving
- Davison's Blueberry Syrup, for serving (optional)

Preheat the barbecue to about 400°F.

In a small saucepan, melt the butter over medium heat. Continue to heat it, swirling it in the pot, until golden brown and nutty, 3–4 minutes.

Halve and pit the apricots. Liberally brush the cut sides with the browned butter and place cut side down on the hot barbecue. Brush the top side with the remaining browned butter. Grill until soft, juicy, and slightly charred, about 3–4 minutes per side.

Pull off the grill and place 2 halves in each dish. Top with a scoop of vanilla ice cream and a drizzle of syrup (if using). Serve immediately. These don't store well.

Chapter 8

Preserves

DAVISON
ORCHARDS
DAVISON

Aprons, Chocolate, and High Heels

My experience with preserving began back in 1979 when I was a newlywed. Although I was working full-time as an interior decorator I was anxious to learn the art of preserving, so I set aside my evenings and my days off to "put up" fruit for the winter. Unlike the generations before me, who preserved the harvest out of necessity, my goal was to use the bounty that God had blessed us with to eat local year-round. You might say I'm a bit of a squirrel by nature and just love to fill my pantry and freezer with good food!

I grew up in Edmonton, where fresh fruit for canning was not available, so the whole concept was very new to me. My mother-in-law, Dora (Nana), has been immersed in preserving since childhood, and I relied on her to teach me. It is probably a mercy that I did not read any canning books or manuals, or I might have been overwhelmed. Rather, I simply met with Dora and watched and learned from her.

As my girls grew up, they expressed an interest in learning to can, so I took on the role of mentor for them. Even my mom got in on the action, driving out from Edmonton to can a year's supply of peaches and tomatoes. The girls wrote a list of "rules" for

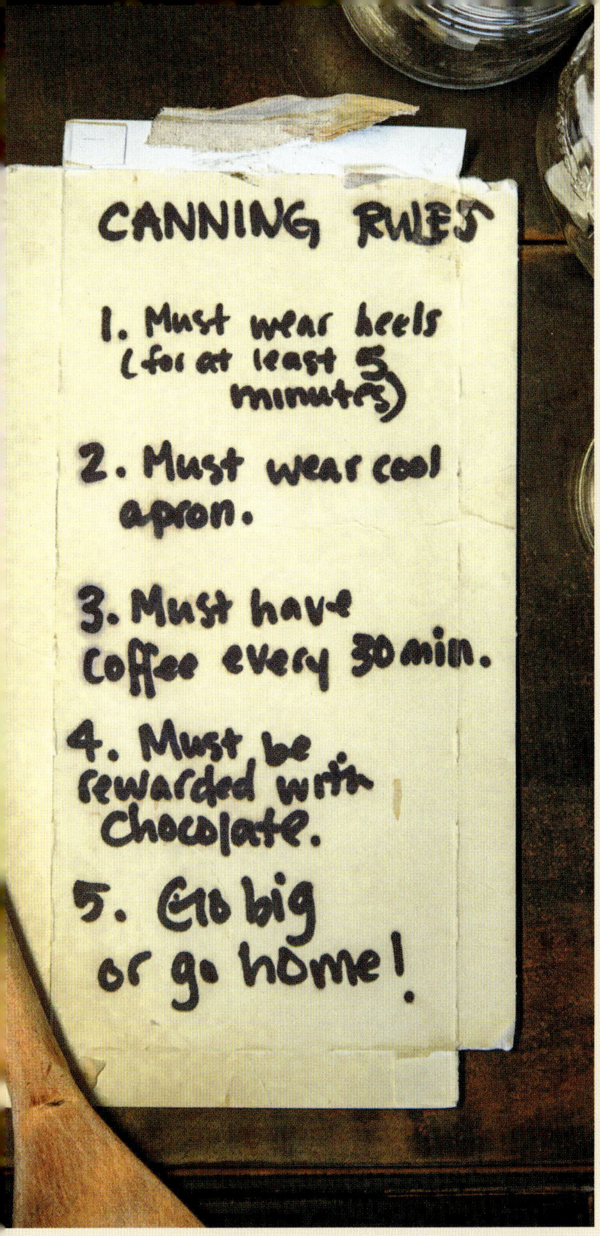

canning: put on fancy aprons and high heels, and indulge in chocolate and coffee while the jars are in the hot-water bath. We sure had some great canning marathons! These are sweet memories I will cherish forever. I still have the precious list of rules tucked away in my tea towel drawer.

It turns out that preserving is a relatively simple and immensely rewarding thing to do, especially if you give yourself enough time. The pop, pop, pop of the lids sealing as the vacuum is created in the jars is still music to my ears. I love seeing my pantry full, knowing I will be able to literally eat the fruits of my labour all winter long and have enough to share with family and friends.

In the following pages you will find our recipes for canned peaches and apricots to offer as a simple dessert, beet and carrot pickles to liven up the supper table, and a selection of delicious and versatile salsas and relishes, jams, and sauces! I am confident that you will find something here to suit your taste. So don your apron, slip on those heels, get out the chocolate, crank the music, and get canning!

Tamra

Canned Apricots

7 pints
20 minutes prep
40 minutes total, plus cooling

"Apricot stuff" is what the Davison Family calls canned apricots that have been puréed into a syrup. Every Sunday morning we enjoy pancakes (page 51) topped with apricot stuff and yogurt for breakfast. If you preserve your apricots in wide-mouth jars, you can purée them with a hand blender and serve them right from the jar! **Tamra**

- 2 cups granulated sugar
- 6 cups water
- 8 lb ripe apricots, rinsed

Sterilize 7 wide-mouth pint jars and lids (see page 8).

In a large saucepan, combine the sugar and water. Bring to a boil over medium-high heat, stirring occasionally. Turn down the heat to low so the mixture stays hot but doesn't keep cooking.

Halve the apricots, remove the pits, and pack them into the prepared jars. Pour the hot syrup over the apricots to just cover them, stopping ½ inch from the rim. Check the jars for air pockets trapped between apricots and the jar wall. Release any air by sliding a butter knife down the side of the jar.

Wipe the rims clean and close each jar with a sterilized lid. Place the jars in a water-filled canner and bring to a full boil. Let them boil in the hot-water bath for 13 minutes, or according to the canning guidelines for your area.

Line your countertop with towels or cutting boards. Using oven mitts and a jar lifter, carefully remove the hot jars from the canner and place them on the towels or cutting boards for 24 hours before storing in a cool dark place for up to 18 months. Once opened, store the jars in the refrigerator and eat the apricots within 2 weeks.

These can be eaten just as they are, with yogurt, or puréed into a syrup as a topping for pancakes or waffles.

Canned Peaches

14 pints
40 minutes prep
1 hour total,
plus cooling

Opening up a jar of home-canned peaches in the dead of winter is like releasing a ray of sunshine and warmth into your frozen world. They are just so summery and fresh! The amounts in this recipe are only guidelines, as there are quite a few variables that can affect the yield. So keep these tips in mind: the basic syrup ratio is 3 cups of water to 1 cup sugar and you need about 2 pounds of peaches to fill a 1-quart jar or 1 pound for a 1-pint jar. Use these basic guidelines to adjust the yield to use up your supplies. **Laura**

---

3 cups granulated sugar
9 cups water
14 lb ripe peaches

Sterilize 14 wide-mouth pint jars and lids (see page 8).

In a large saucepan, combine the sugar and water. Bring to a boil over medium-high heat, stirring occasionally. Turn down the heat to low so the mixture stays hot but doesn't keep cooking.

Bring a large pot of water to a boil over high heat and prepare a bowl of ice water. Working in batches, place the peaches in the boiling water for about 30 seconds and then transfer them to the ice water. This will help to loosen the peel. Slide the peel off the peaches and slice them into the prepared jars. Pour the hot syrup over the peaches to just cover them, stopping ½ inch from the rim. Check the jars for air pockets trapped between peaches and the jar wall. Release any air by sliding a butter knife down the side of the jar.

Wipe the rims clean and close each jar with a sterilized lid. Place the jars in a water-filled canner and bring to a full boil. Let them boil in the hot-water bath for 15 minutes, or according to the canning guidelines for your area.

Line your countertop with towels or cutting boards. Using oven mitts and a jar lifter, carefully remove the hot jars from the canner and place them on the towels or cutting boards for 24 hours before storing in a cool dark place for up to 2 years. Once opened, store the jars in the refrigerator and eat the peaches within 2 weeks.

These can be enjoyed on their own, with ice cream, or on top of baked oatmeal (page 69). You can also use them in Okanagan Baked Chicken (page 141).

Grandma Quast's Pickled Beets

7 pints
35 minutes prep
2 hours total,
plus cooling

Sweet yet savoury, this amazing pickled beets recipe has been handed down in our family from Tamra's mom, Olive "Gigi" Quast. When her grandkids were starting to grow up and move out, Gigi started a tradition of giving canned produce as Christmas presents. We could order 12 jars from a list of options, and I always asked for at least six jars of these beets! When she was no longer able to keep up the tradition, I made sure to get this recipe from her. Making them always makes me think of how generous and hard-working Gigi is. **Rachel**

---

7 lb whole beets
2 cups granulated sugar
2 cups water
2 cups white vinegar
1 Tbsp ground cinnamon
1 tsp ground allspice
1 tsp ground cloves

Note: Serve your pickled beets as a side on your dinner plate or sliced in a fresh garden salad. They are a must-have at our Thanksgiving and Christmas dinners.

Sterilize 7 pint jars (wide-mouth or standard) and lids (see page 8).

Place the whole beets in a large pot and cover with water. Bring to a boil over high heat and then turn down to medium-low to simmer until the beets are cooked through and can easily be pierced with a fork, about 1 hour.

Prepare an ice bath and place the cooked beets in it. Stem, peel, then cut the beets into approximately 1-inch pieces.

Pack the beet pieces into the prepared jars.

In a large pot over high heat, bring the sugar, water, vinegar, cinnamon, allspice, and cloves to a rolling boil, and then remove from the heat. Pour the hot brine over the beets, stopping ½ inch from the top of the jar. Check the jars for air pockets trapped between beets and the jar wall. Release any air by sliding a butter knife down the side of the jar.

Wipe the rims clean and close each jar with a sterilized lid. Place the jars in a water-filled canner and bring to a full boil. Let them boil in the hot-water bath for 15 minutes, or according to the canning guidelines for your area.

Line your countertop with towels or cutting boards. Using oven mitts and a jar lifter, carefully remove the hot jars from the canner and place them on the towels or cutting boards for 24 hours before storing in a cool dark place. Allow the pickled beets to cure for 2 months before enjoying.

Store in the refrigerator after opening for up to 4 weeks. Sealed jars last in the pantry for up to 18 months.

Ripe Watermelon Pickles
1 cup sugar
1 cup vinegar
1 tbsp. salt
1 not too ripe watermelon
Cut the rind off slices of the watermelon, cut the rest into strips or chunks. Fill sterilized jars with the pieces. To each jar add a sprig or two of dill. Bring syrup to a boil and cook a few minutes, pour over pickles and seal. Steam in boiling water 5 minutes to seal jars.
Mrs. J. Steingart, Steinbach, Man.
Watermelon Pickles
1 gal. watermelon ripe or semi-ripe. peel and cut in small pieces
1 cup vinegar
1 tbsp. salt
4 tbsp. sugar
Bring syrup to boil, then add the cut watermelon. Bring to a boil. Put a sprig of dill in each jar, and then fill with pickles. Seal.
Mrs. P. Olfert, Steinbach, Man.
from the tomatoes
6 large onions
1 bunch celery
1 bunch parsley or 5 parsley roots
6 sweet peppers
3 bay leaves
Cut celery, peppers, onions and parsley roots in small pieces. Add these with the bay leaves to the strained tomatoes and boil steadily for 2 hours. Now add:
1/2 cup sugar
5 tbsp. salt
3/4 cup flour
1/2 cup butter
1/4 tsp. cayenne
Melt butter, add flour and make a paste with some tomato sauce. Add to other ingredients. Bring to boil and fill jars. Seal immediately.
Ikra
4 big egg plants
20 large tomatoes
20 - 25 carrots
1 bunch celery, cut fine
10 large onions
2 sweet peppers, chopped
1 small red pepper (hot)
1 cup sugar
Salt and pepper to taste
1 cup cooking or olive oil

Pickled Carrots

9 pints
1 hour prep
1 hour, 10 minutes total, plus cooling

Another classic recipe from Gigi, these carrots are gorgeous in the jar and simple to make. They pack a punch, though, so if you are not a lover of heat or you have small children, you may want to pare back the cayenne a bit. **Laura**

- 9 small dill heads plus at least 9 dill fronds
- 1 small yellow onion, cut into 9 slices
- 8 lb carrots
- 4 cups water
- 4 cups white vinegar
- ½ cup pickling salt
- ½ cup granulated sugar
- ½–1 tsp cayenne pepper (depending on your taste)

Sterilize 9 pint jars (wide-mouth or standard) and lids (see page 8).

Place 1 dill head and 1 or 2 dill fronds into each clean, sterilized pint jar. Add 1 onion slice. Peel the carrots and cut them into ¼-inch-thick fingers at least ½ inch shorter than the height of the jars. Pack them into the jars.

In a large saucepan bring the water, vinegar, salt, sugar, and cayenne to a boil over medium-high heat, stirring occasionally. Turn down the heat to low so the mixture stays hot but doesn't keep cooking. Pour the hot brine over the carrots, stopping ½ inch from the rim. Check the jars for air pockets trapped between the carrots and the jar wall. Release any air by sliding a butter knife down the side of the jar.

Wipe the rims clean and close each jar with a sterilized lid. Place the jars in a water-filled canner and bring to a full boil. Let them boil in the hot-water bath for 10 minutes, or according to the canning guidelines for your area.

Line your countertop with towels or cutting boards. Using oven mitts and a jar lifter, carefully remove the hot jars from the canner and place them on the towels or cutting boards for 24 hours before storing in a cool dark place for up to 18 months. Allow the pickles to cure for 1 month before eating.

Keep opened jars in the refrigerator for up to 4 weeks.

These take any meal to the next level. Serve them at an appetizer party or plate them along with Grandma Quast's Pickled Beets (page 235).

Fresh Salsa: Peach or Tomato

4 cups salsa
15 minutes prep
15 minutes total

Nothing says summer like this fresh salsa. You can make it with fresh-from-the-field Roma tomatoes or with juicy peaches. I highly recommend you make a batch of both! If you want to increase the spice, use the seeds of your jalapeño. **Laura**

- 3 cups peeled, pitted, and chopped peaches, or chopped Roma tomatoes
- ½ cup diced white onion
- 1 clove garlic, crushed and minced
- ⅓ cup chopped cilantro
- 1–2 jalapeños, deseeded and diced (leave seeds in for a spicier salsa)
- ¼ cup freshly squeezed lime juice (2–3 limes)
- 1 Tbsp ground cumin
- 1 tsp chili powder
- 1 tsp sea salt

In a serving bowl, combine the fruit, onion, garlic, cilantro, and jalapeños.

In a glass measuring cup, stir together the lime juice, cumin, chili powder, and salt. Pour this over the vegetable mixture and stir to combine.

Enjoy with chips, on crostinis, on chicken, or however and wherever you like to enjoy salsa.

Leftovers can be stored in an airtight container in the refrigerator for up to 4 days.

A FARM FAVOURITE

Apple Salsa

14 pints
1 hour prep
(if chopping by hand)
2¼ hours total,
plus cooling

The name of this salsa is a little bit misleading. Although it is full of apples, it does not taste like apples and you don't notice them in the final product. They play a key role, however, as they thicken the salsa and intensify the sweet yet surprisingly spicy flavour. This is my family's favourite salsa by a long shot. **Rachel**

- 12 cups chopped Roma tomatoes, blanched and peeled if desired
- 12 cups diced yellow onion
- 8 medium apples, cored and grated (peeled if desired, see note)
- 3 jalapeños, deseeded and chopped (leave seeds in for a spicier salsa)
- 6 cloves garlic, crushed and minced
- 3 green bell peppers, deseeded and chopped
- 3 red or yellow bell peppers, deseeded and chopped
- 2 cups white vinegar
- 5 Tbsp coarse salt
- 1½ tsp paprika
- 1½ tsp dried mustard
- 2 tsp ground cayenne pepper
- 3 (each 5½ oz/156 mL) cans tomato paste

Note: Mild, thin-skinned apples that cook down easily are preferable for this recipe. I like to use Sunrise, Silken, Golden Delicious, or Aurora. If your apple choice has a tougher skin (such as McIntosh) peeling them would be advisable.

In a large stock pot, combine the tomatoes, onions, apples, jalapeños, garlic, bell peppers, and vinegar.

Bring to a gentle boil over medium-low heat, and cook, stirring frequently, until the onions are translucent and the garlic is vibrant white, about 1 hour.

Add the salt, paprika, dried mustard, cayenne pepper, and tomato paste. Increase the heat to medium to bring it back to a boil, stirring often, and boil for 3 minutes.

Sterilize 14 pint jars (wide-mouth or standard) and lids (see page 8). Working with one jar at a time, ladle the salsa into the jars, stopping ½ inch from the rim. Check the jars for air pockets trapped between the salsa and the jar wall. Release any air by sliding a butter knife down the side of the jar.

Wipe the rims clean and close each jar with a sterilized lid. Place the jars in a water-filled canner and bring to a full boil. Let them boil in the hot-water bath for 15 minutes, or according to the canning guidelines of your area.

Line your countertop with towels or cutting boards. Using oven mitts and a jar lifter, carefully remove the hot jars from the canner and place them on the towels or cutting boards for 24 hours before storing in a cool dark place for up to 1 year.

If any jars do not seal, put them in the refrigerator and use them within 4 weeks. Enjoy this salsa piled high on grilled cheese or quesadillas, use it as a cheater enchilada sauce, or eat it with tortilla chips.

A FARM FAVOURITE

DAVISON ORCHARDS
Cannery
Okanagan
Summer Salsa
salsa d'été d'Okanagan
- 375ml -

Okanagan Summer Salsa

10 pints
1 hour prep
(if chopping by hand)
2¼ hours total,
plus cooling

Filled with the goodness of late summer, this cooked salsa is the one to make if you are looking for a classic, traditional condiment. Tom and I count this as our favourite salsa. I make it every year. **Tamra**

- 12 cups chopped Roma tomatoes, blanched and peeled if desired
- 2 green bell peppers, deseeded and chopped
- 2 red bell peppers, deseeded and chopped
- 2 yellow bell peppers, deseeded and chopped
- 2 orange bell peppers, deseeded and chopped
- 4½ cups chopped yellow onions
- 4–5 jalapeños, deseeded and chopped (leave seeds in for a spicier salsa)
- 6 cloves garlic, crushed and minced
- 4 (each 5½ oz/156 mL) cans tomato paste
- 3 cups white vinegar
- 3 Tbsp granulated sugar
- 1½ Tbsp coarse salt
- 1½ Tbsp paprika
- 1½ tsp dried oregano

In a large stock pot, combine the tomatoes, peppers, onions, jalapeños, and garlic. Mix in the tomato paste, vinegar, sugar, salt, paprika, and oregano.

Bring to a boil over medium-high heat, turn down the heat to low, and simmer, stirring occasionally, until the onions are translucent, the garlic is vibrant white and the salsa has thickened to your liking, about 1 hour.

Sterilize 10 pint jars (wide-mouth or standard) and lids (see page 8). Working with one jar at a time, ladle the salsa into the jars, stopping ½ inch from the rim. Check the jars for air pockets trapped between the salsa and the jar wall. Release any air by sliding a butter knife down the side of the jar.

Wipe the rims clean and close each jar with a sterilized lid. Place the jars in a water-filled canner and bring to a full boil. Let them boil in the hot-water bath for 15 minutes, or according to the canning guidelines of your area.

Line your countertop with towels or cutting boards. Using oven mitts and a jar lifter, carefully remove the hot jars from the canner and place them on the towels or cutting boards for 24 hours before storing in a cool dark place for up to 1 year.

If any jars do not seal, put them in the refrigerator and use them within 4 weeks.

Enjoy this salsa with a big bag of tortilla chips, alongside scrambled eggs, or piled on a baked potato.

A FARM FAVOURITE

Loads of Herbs Tomato Sauce

About 10 cups sauce
30 minutes prep
2½ hours total

Nothing compares to a sun-ripened tomato, and for about five weeks of the year our farm has an endless supply of these gems. As a newlywed, I made it my mission to develop a tomato sauce recipe that showcased this truly abundant, yet extremely seasonal, ingredient. This recipe is bursting with flavour and, as its name suggests, is loaded with herbs. It freezes well, so you can make big batches of it and stow it away for an easy supper on a busy day. **Laura**

---

2 Tbsp olive oil
5 cups diced white onions
6 cloves garlic, crushed and minced
5 lb Roma tomatoes
4 bay leaves
2 Tbsp dried basil
4 tsp dried oregano
3 tsp dried parsley
1 tsp salt
½ tsp pepper
1 (5½ oz/156 mL) can tomato paste

Note: If you prefer to use fresh herbs, simply double the amount and add them during the last 30 minutes of cooking.

In a large pot over medium heat, warm the oil. Sauté the onions and garlic until soft, about 5 minutes.

Meanwhile, bring a large pot of water to a boil. Fill a large bowl with ice water. Working in batches, immerse the tomatoes in the boiling water for about 45 seconds, then plunge into the ice water. Slide the peels off, quarter the tomatoes, and add to the pot with the onions.

Mix in the bay leaves and all the herbs, the salt, and the pepper. Cook, uncovered and stirring frequently, until the tomatoes have reduced and broken down into a nice sauce consistency, about 1½ hours. Remove the bay leaves. Mix in the tomato paste and cook, stirring frequently, until the sauce is nicely thickened, about 10 more minutes. Adjust the seasonings to taste. If you prefer a smoother sauce, purée it with a hand blender or traditional blender.

Store in an airtight container in the refrigerator for up to 5 days, or freeze in serving-size portions for up to 6 months.

This tomato sauce shines on its own with a big bowl of pasta but can also be used as homemade sauce for Rachel's Spaghetti Squash Lasagna (page 157).

Roasted Roma Tomatoes

3½–4 cups
15 minutes prep
2 hours, 45 minutes total

This recipe is another Davison Family classic. We make this in huge batches, cramming our ovens as full as possible until the whole house (and everyone in it) is permeated with the smell of garlic, onions, and tomatoes. Roasted Romas freeze beautifully for months, so when the tomatoes hit their peak season, it's time to get roasting! **Tamra**

- 3 lb Roma tomatoes, washed and quartered
- 2 cups chopped yellow onions
- 2 cloves garlic, minced
- 3 Tbsp fresh basil, roughly chopped
- 2 Tbsp olive oil
- ½ tsp salt
- ½ tsp pepper

Preheat the oven to 350°F. Line an 11 × 15-inch glass baking pan (or 2 smaller ones) with parchment paper.

In a large bowl, mix together the tomatoes, onions, garlic, and basil. Drizzle the oil overtop and toss to combine. Season with the salt and pepper, stirring one more time.

Spread the tomato mixture evenly in the pan. Bake, uncovered, for 2–2½ hours, stirring every ½ hour or so. Once most of the liquid has evaporated and the vegetables are all very soft, your roasted Romas are ready.

Store in an airtight container in the refrigerator for up to 4 days or in the freezer for up to 1 year.

Serve over pasta for a quick and easy, flavourful meal, on toasted baguettes for an impressive bruschetta, or puréed for an astonishing pizza sauce.

crafted for quality
sealed for freshness

Lady Rose Relish

5–6 pints
2–3 hours prep
12 hours total,
plus cooling

This relish has a serious reputation around our farm. Because of the turmeric, vinegar, and mustard seed, it produces a very strong, unmistakable aroma when it's being cooked. As a result, the whole Davison team knows when it's Lady Rose Relish Week in the Cannery. But this beautiful, bright, and tangy relish also has a serious reputation with our guests. They can't get enough! Once you've tried this relish you'll never go back. **Laura**

- 4 cups thinly chopped celery
- 3 cups diced coloured bell peppers (mix of red, yellow, and/or green)
- 2 cups peeled and diced field or English cucumbers
- 2 cups diced yellow onions
- 1 jalapeño, deseeded and diced
- ¼ cup coarse salt
- 3 cups granulated sugar
- 1 Tbsp yellow mustard seeds
- 2½ cups white vinegar, divided
- ⅓ cup all-purpose flour
- 1½ tsp ground turmeric

Note: This relish tastes amazing served with baked ham, on hot dogs, or with sausages.

In a large bowl, mix the vegetables with the salt. Dump it all into a colander and set the colander in the bowl. Cover the bowl with plastic wrap and refrigerate overnight to drain.

The next morning, sterilize 6 pint jars (wide-mouth or standard) and lids (see page 8).

Place the drained vegetables in a large pot. Add the sugar, mustard seeds, and 2 cups of the vinegar. Bring to a boil slowly over medium heat, stirring regularly. Turn down the heat to low and simmer the vegetables until the celery is tender but not mushy, 7–10 minutes.

In a glass measuring cup, whisk the remaining ½ cup of vinegar with the flour and turmeric until no lumps remain. Stirring constantly, slowly pour the flour mixture into the pot and cook over low heat until thickened and clear, about 5–10 minutes.

Working with one jar at a time, ladle the relish into the jars, stopping ½ inch from the rim. Wipe the rims clean and close each jar with a sterilized lid. Place the jars in a water-filled canner and bring to a full boil. Let them boil in the hot-water bath for 10 minutes, or according to the canning guidelines of your area.

Line your countertop with towels or cutting boards. Using oven mitts and a jar lifter, carefully remove the hot jars from the canner and place them on the towels or cutting boards for 24 hours before storing in a cool, dark place for up to 18 months. Store in the refrigerator and use within 1 month once opened.

A FARM FAVOURITE

Apricot Jam

Five ½-pint jars
30 minutes prep
30 minutes total,
plus 24 hrs to set

Apricot jam is Nana Davison's all-time favourite, and it's no wonder. I don't think it has an equal when it comes to colour and intenseness of flavour. I'll be honest, though: I was never a fan of apricot jam until I stumbled upon this recipe in one of my grandma's antiquated cookbooks. Now I am hooked! **Rachel**

- 2½ lb ripe apricots
- 3 cups granulated sugar
- 1 Tbsp lemon juice

Sterilize five ½-pint jars (wide-mouth or standard) and lids (see page 8).

Wash, pit, and finely chop the apricots until you have enough to measure 4 cups of prepared fruit.

In a large stock pot, stir together the apricots, sugar, and lemon juice. Place the pot over medium-high heat and cook the mixture rapidly, stirring until it reaches its jelly point. This should take about 10–15 minutes of boiling.

To test for the jelly point, dip a clean stainless steel spoon into the jam pot. If the jam congeals immediately on the spoon, it has reached its jelly point. If it hasn't reached its jelly point, cook it for another 3–5 minutes, stirring rapidly, and test again.

Line your countertop with towels or cutting boards.

Working with one jar at a time, ladle the jam into the jars, stopping ½ inch from the rim.

Wipe the rims clean and close each jar with a sterilized lid.

Place filled jars on the towels or cutting boards for 24 hours before storing in a cool dark place for up to 1 year. Refrigerate after opening for up to 4 weeks.

Enjoy this jam on your morning toast or spread thinly on a freshly made crêpe.

Rhubarb Jam

2 cups
25 minutes prep
40 minutes total

When I was growing up on the prairies, rhubarb was a staple in our diet. My mom would make this rhubarb jam in huge batches. It is delicious served on toast or in a PB-and-J sandwich, but it can also be stirred into yogurt or served as a sauce alongside a pork tenderloin. **Rachel**

---

4 cups chopped rhubarb stalks
1 cup granulated sugar

Note: 4 cups of rhubarb to 1 cup of sugar is the ratio to keep in mind when you're making this jam. With that knowledge you can make your batches as big or as small as you like, bearing in mind that the cooking time will need to increase as your batch size increases.

In a large saucepan, mix together the rhubarb and sugar. Stir and allow to sit for 15 minutes to allow the rhubarb to release some juice. This will keep your jam from burning easily.

Place the pot over medium-high heat and bring to a boil, stirring frequently. Turn down the heat to medium-low and simmer for about 15 minutes, stirring constantly, until the jam is thickened, sticks to the spoon, and splatters while it simmers. Remove from the heat and let cool in the pot.

Pour the jam into freezer-safe containers and store in the refrigerator for up to 1 month or the freezer for up to 1 year.

Use this as a traditional jam or enjoy it warm over vanilla ice cream.

Applesauce

About 4–5 cups
20 minutes prep
2 hours, 20 minutes total

People often ask us how to make homemade applesauce, so we are including it here because we believe that it's an essential life skill! For those of you who already know the basics of applesauce making, we are including a few fun variations to jazz it up a little. I never add sugar to my applesauce. The apples I use are sweet, so extra sugar is just not necessary. If you use tarter apples, feel free to add sugar to taste. **Rachel**

Classic Applesauce

10 apples (Mutsu, Honeycrisp, Golden Delicious, McIntosh, or a blend of these works well)
2 Tbsp water

Plum-Applesauce

8 apples
8 prune plums, pitted
2 Tbsp water
1 tsp vanilla extract (optional)

Apples 'n' Spice Sauce

10 apples
2 Tbsp water
½ tsp ground cinnamon
⅛ tsp ground cloves
⅛ tsp ground nutmeg
1 Tbsp granulated sugar

Pear-Applesauce

6 apples
4 pears
2 Tbsp water
1 Tbsp lemon juice

Note: We love applesauce on its own as a snack, as a side with pork tenderloin, or as a special treat topped with whipped cream!

If prepping by hand

Peel and core the fruit. Cut it into evenly sized pieces and place in a large, heavy pot. Add the water. This keeps the fruit from burning before it releases its juices.

Place the pot over medium-low heat and cook, stirring occasionally, until the fruit is broken down and soft, about 2 hours. Add more water, 1 Tbsp at a time, if needed throughout cooking. Add spices, vanilla, or lemon juice, if listed in the recipe, during the last 10 minutes of cooking.

Mash with a potato masher or purée smooth with a hand blender. Let cool and serve.

If using a food mill

If you own a food mill, there is no need to peel or core the fruit (but pits must be removed from plums). Simply roughly chop the fruit and place it in a heavy pot.

Add the water and cook over medium-low heat, stirring occasionally, until the fruit is broken down and soft, about 2 hours. Add more water, 1 Tbsp at a time, if needed throughout cooking. Add spices, vanilla, or lemon juice, if listed in recipe, during the last 10 minutes of cooking.

Working in batches, put the cooked fruit through the food mill. The seeds, core, and skin will be removed and you will be left with an applesauce of perfect consistency. Let cool and serve.

Applesauce can be kept in an airtight container in the refrigerator for 1 week or frozen for up to 4 months.

Chapter 9

Beverages

FORD
DAVISON
ORCHARDS
VERNON, B.

The Four Seasons

We Davisons grew up on the farm, so we truly think and live seasonally. Maybe it's because we spend so much of our time outdoors, or because there are four very distinct seasons, each three months long, in the Okanagan Valley, which we are blessed to call home. Whatever the reason, our chores change with the seasons, our business changes with the seasons, and in the kitchen the menu changes with the seasons. Each season sees us adapt different patterns and habits to fit that particular time of year. Some of our behaviours are no doubt habitual. We do the things we grew up doing because that's what we've always done. Some habits, however, are definitely brought on by the changing of the seasons. I truly believe that the weather has a deep effect on our psyche. It impacts our mood and influences what we want to eat and drink.

While we all know it's important to drink plenty of water every day, it's fun to enjoy a few homemade, seasonal drinks as well! In this closing chapter we share a few family favourites. They are simple, family-friendly beverages that complement the seasons and are straightforward to make at home.

When the snow melts and the first fruits of the season are budding, we crave all things strawberry and rhubarb. In the long days of July and the heat of the summer, nothing is more refreshing than an icy-cold glass of Laura's Peach Iced Tea (page 263) on the deck. When the farm is bustling with the apple harvest and the temperatures dip down below zero for the first time, nothing tastes better than a steaming cup of Spiced Apple Cider (page 275). And in January, when the wind is howling and the snow is swirling, a cup of rich Homemade Hot Chocolate (page 273) not only is comforting but also has a way of warming up the whole room.

Enjoy adding a seasonal drink to the menu as a symbol of each season, allowing the seasons to subtly impact your habits and routines. You may find it brings a fun variation to your menu planning, and encourages you to take advantage of what each season has to offer.

Laura

KEEPER
of the
PATCH
Canada

Laura's Peach Iced Tea

8 cups
10 minutes prep
10 minutes total, plus chilling

I love real iced tea, but for years I struggled to find a recipe that was just right for me. Over time, with much trial and error, I developed this one. I am known to always have a pitcher of it on hand during the warm months. The lemon juice is the not-so-secret ingredient that really makes it thirst-quenching! **Laura**

- 2 cups freshly boiled water
- 2 black tea bags
- 2 herbal peach tea bags
- ½ cup granulated sugar
- 6 cups cold water
- ½ cup lemon juice (3–4 lemons)
- Ice cubes, for serving

Place the freshly boiled water in a large serving jug. Add all 4 tea bags and steep for 5–7 minutes.

Discard the tea bags. Add the sugar to the hot tea and stir until dissolved. Add the cold water and lemon juice. Stir.

Chill in your refrigerator until cold, at least 2 hours. Serve over ice.

This can be kept in an airtight container in your refrigerator for up to 1 month. Stir well before serving.

A FARM FAVOURITE

Real Fruit Milkshakes

Serves 4
10 minutes prep
10 minutes total

Is there a better summer treat than a milkshake made with fresh fruit? I don't think there is. This simple recipe is totally versatile. I enjoy a classic strawberry milkshake. Peach is a nice surprise, and cherry feels fancy. You can really use any berry or soft fruit that you have on hand! **Rachel**

---

2 cups fresh or frozen fruit or berries
4 cups vanilla ice cream
1½ tsp vanilla extract
1 cup milk

Prepare your fruit by hulling, pitting, peeling, and/or chopping, depending on what fruit or berry you are using.

Dump all of the ingredients into a blender in the order listed. Blend until smooth.

Pour into glasses and serve immediately.

Rhubarb Slush

6 cups
15 minutes prep
35 minutes total,
plus freezing

This is an old Prairie recipe, and when I was a child it seemed like everyone's grandma had a pail of it in their freezers to pull out for the grandkids on a hot summer day. If you'd like to just make rhubarb juice, omit the Jell-O and 7UP and follow the first step. **Rachel**

---

6 cups chopped rhubarb stalks
1½ cups granulated sugar
6 cups water
⅓ cup lemon juice (about 3 lemons)
1 box (85 g) strawberry Jell-O jelly powder
7UP, for serving

Place the rhubarb, sugar, water, and lemon juice in a heavy stock pot. Bring to a boil over medium heat and simmer for 10–15 minutes, or until the rhubarb is very soft. Carefully pour the mixture through a fine mesh strainer set over a large glass bowl to catch the juice. Discard the pulp.

Stir the Jell-O into the hot rhubarb juice until dissolved. Pour into a freezer-safe container and freeze for at least 12 hours before serving. This can be kept in the freezer for up to 8 months.

To serve, fill a glass about half full with rhubarb slush. Pour 7UP over the slush and enjoy. Alternatively, serve the slush on its own as a sorbet!

Sparkling Cherry Lemonade

8 cups
10 minutes prep
10 minutes total, plus chilling

Looking for a special beverage for your pool party or Canada Day celebration? Look no further! This pleasantly sweet treat hits the spot on a warm day. If you'd rather add the soda water to individual cups, a 50:50 ratio is about right. **Tamra**

- 2 cups pitted sweet cherries
- 1 cup granulated sugar
- 1 cup lemon juice (5–6 lemons)
- 2 cups cold water
- 4 cups soda water
- 8 sweet cherries, for garnish (optional)

Place the pitted cherries, sugar, and lemon juice in a blender or a food processor fitted with the steel blade. Blend until smooth. Pour into a pitcher or large jar, add the cold water, and place in the refrigerator to chill. This step can be done a day in advance.

When you're ready to serve, give the jar a shake, or give the liquid a good stir, and mix in the soda water. Pour into glasses and garnish the rim with a whole cherry if desired.

Rae's Iced Coffee

Serves 8
5 minutes prep
5 minutes total, plus chilling

Calling all coffee lovers! This iced coffee is incredibly simple to make and the concentrate can be kept in your refrigerator for that moment when you are craving caffeine but it's too hot for a coffee. **Laura**

½ cup instant coffee
½ cup granulated sugar
½ cup freshly boiled water
Ice, for serving
Milk, for serving

In a glass jar with a lid, stir together the instant coffee, sugar, and water until the sugar is dissolved. Refrigerate until cold, at least 3 hours. This concentrate can be kept in the refrigerator for up to 1 month.

When you are ready to serve, half fill a glass with ice. Top with 2 Tbsp of the coffee concentrate and 1 cup of milk. Stir and enjoy!

A FARM FAVOURITE

Homemade Hot Chocolate

Serves 4
10 minutes prep
10 minutes total

Every December our family goes out to the backwoods on a Christmas tree hunt with some of our closest friends. We build a fire, roast hot dogs, cut down the "perfect" tree, and enjoy friendly snowball fights. The festivities are never complete without a steaming cup of hot chocolate piled high with whipped cream! **Rachel**

- 4 cups milk
- ¼ cup cocoa powder
- ¼ cup granulated sugar
- ⅓ cup semisweet chocolate chips
- ½ tsp vanilla extract
- Whipped cream, for serving (optional)
- Crushed candy canes, for serving (optional)

In a heavy saucepan over medium heat, whisk together the milk, cocoa powder, and sugar. Heat until almost boiling but don't let it reach a boil.

Remove from the heat and stir in the chocolate chips until melted and smooth. Stir in the vanilla.

Pour into mugs and top with whipped cream and crushed candy canes (if using). This is best served right away. If you are putting it in a thermos for later, be sure to give it a good shake before serving as the chocolate will have settled (and don't add the whipped cream or the candy canes until you're ready to drink it).

Spiced Apple Cider

7 cups
5 minutes prep
2–3 hours total

When you are chilled to the bone, I can think of nothing in the world that will warm you from the inside out like a steaming hot mug of spiced apple cider. If you don't have a crock pot, mull the cider over low heat in a pot on the stove for 2 hours. Be careful not to let it boil, as the juice will separate. If that happens, though, do not fret. It's not a disaster. It won't look as good, but it will taste the same! **Tamra**

- 1 (1.8 L) jug Davison's Pure Apple Juice
- 2 tsp whole allspice
- 1 tsp whole cloves
- ½ tsp dried orange peel pieces
- 3 cinnamon sticks

Pour the apple juice into a crock pot and set it to medium (or high, if your crock pot only has 2 options).

Place the allspice, cloves, and orange peel in a tea bag or infuser. Add to the apple juice, along with the cinnamon sticks.

Mull for 2–3 hours. The longer it mulls, the stronger it will be. Remove and discard the spices. Serve warm.

Leftover cider can be kept in an airtight jar in the refrigerator for up to 4 weeks. Reheat to serve.

A FARM FAVOURITE

Gratitude

The writing of this book has been a huge undertaking and would not have been possible without the help of many people.

First of all, Callum. Thank you for your endless patience, your fabulous photography skills, your go-with-the-flow positivity—and did I mention your endless patience?! You put up with us calling you over at every hour to snap a photograph or two. Thank you for enduring the dog trying to taste-test every dish, the weather blowing our props around, the children yelling "Ca-Ca, look at me!!" and us looking over your shoulder. You're one of a kind.

Tom, Kevin, and Lance, our dear husbands: You've put up with a lot. What can we say but thank you for being gracious and supportive and for loving us through our ups and downs.

To our precious children, thank you for being our number one taste-testers and for your blunt and honest feedback. Thank you for your patience in sharing your moms a little more than usual.

To each of our mothers and grandmothers, thank you for teaching us to cook, for passing your wisdom down through the generations, for walking us through the documentation of never-been-written family recipes, and for sharing with us the value of home cooking.

Nana, you are the inspiration for this book. So many of the recipes are ones that you lovingly made for us year after year.

Raelene, you've shared your years of experience, your recipes, and your life and time with us. Thank you for being our friend, mentor, and second mom.

Leah, your willingness to listen and advise through thick and thin has not gone unnoticed. Thank you for sharing many of your exceptional recipes with us. We love you, sister.

To our loyal customers and followers, thank you for encouraging us, supporting us, and visiting our farm. Without you, there would be no cookbook or Davison Orchards.

Nancy Wise, thank you for taking the time to talk us through what it means to publish a book. Your insight, experience, and wisdom were invaluable. Thank you also for passing on our proposal and putting in a good word for us. We could not have done this without you.

Karlynn Johnston, as we fumbled around trying to get started, you took time out of your busy life to talk, share your wisdom, and get us pointed in the right direction. Thank you for your generosity in teaching us how to write a proposal and for your valuable feedback.

Tori and the TouchWood team, thank you for choosing to work with us to get this book into people's hands.

Above all, we would like to acknowledge the work of God in our lives: Thank you for creating us, for saving us, and for graciously allowing us to live and enjoy life, good food, family, friends, and land to farm. All the praise and glory goes to you!

Rachel, Tamra, and Laura

DAVISON

W&W

METRIC CONVERSION CHART

VOLUME

Imperial	Metric
⅛ tsp	0.5 mL
¼ tsp	1 mL
½ tsp	2.5 mL
¾ tsp	4 mL
1 tsp	5 mL
½ Tbsp	8 mL
1 Tbsp	15 mL
1½ Tbsp	23 mL
2 Tbsp	30 mL
2½ Tbsp	38 mL
¼ cup	60 mL
⅓ cup	80 mL
½ cup	125 mL
⅔ cup	165 mL
¾ cup	185 mL
1 cup	250 mL
1¼ cups	310 mL
1⅓ cups	330 mL
1½ cups	375 mL
1⅔ cups	415 mL
1¾ cups	435 mL
2 cups/ 1 pint	500 mL
2¼ cups	560 mL
2⅓ cups	580 mL
2½ cups	625 mL
2⅔ cups	665 mL
2¾ cups	690 mL
3 cups	750 mL
3½ cups	875 mL
4 cups	1 L
5 cups	1.25 L
6 cups	1.5 L
8 cups / 2 quarts	2 L
25 cups	6 L

WEIGHT

Imperial	Metric
1 oz	30 g
4 oz	115 g
8 oz	225 g
10 oz	250 g
12 oz	340 g
1 lb (16 oz)	450 g
2 lb	900 g
5 lb	2,250 g

CANS

Imperial	Metric
6 oz	177mL
10 oz	284 mL
11oz	300ml
14 oz	398 mL
16 oz	480 mL
28 oz	796 mL

LENGTH / WIDTH

Imperial	Metric
1⁄12 inch	2 mm
⅛ inch	3 mm
⅙ inch	4 mm
¼ inch	6 mm
½ inch	12 mm
¾ inch	2 cm
1 inch	2.5 cm
1½ inches	3.5 cm
2 inches	5 cm
2½ inches	6.5 cm
3 inches	7.5 cm
3½ inches	9 cm
4 inches	10 cm
5 inches	12.5 cm
6 inches	15 cm
7 inches	18 cm
8 inches	20 cm
9 inches	23 cm
10 inches	25 cm

TEMPERATURE

(For oven temperatures, see chart below)

Imperial	Metric
115°F	46°C
150°F	66°C
160°F	71°C
170°F	77°C
180°F	82°C
185°F	85°C
190°F	88°C
200°F	93°C
240°F	116°C
247°F	119°C
250°F	121°C
290°F	143°C
300°F	149°C
350°F	177°C
360°F	182°C
370°F	188°C

OVEN TEMPERATURE

Imperial	Metric
200°F	95°C
225°F	105°C
250°F	120°C
275°F	135°C
300°F	150°C
325°F	160°C
350°F	180°C
375°F	190°C
400°F	200°C
425°F	220°C
450°F	230°C

US FLUID OUNCES

US fluid ounces	US customary	Metric
¼ oz	½ Tbsp / 1½ tsp	7.5 mL
⅓ oz	2 tsp	10 mL
½ oz	1 Tbsp	15 mL
¾ oz	1½ Tbsp / 4½ tsp	22 mL
1 oz (1 shot)	2 Tbsp	30 mL
1¼ oz	2½ Tbsp	37.5 mL
1½ oz	3 Tbsp	45 mL
2 oz	¼ cup	60 mL
2½ oz	5 Tbsp	75 mL
3 oz	¼ cup + 2 Tbsp	90 mL
3½ oz	¼ cup + 3 Tbsp	105 mL
4 oz	½ cup	125 mL
4½ oz	½ cup + 1 Tbsp	140 mL
5 oz	½ cup + 2 Tbsp	155 mL

INDEX

P

NOTES

NOTES

TouchWood Editions
touchwoodeditions.com

Edited by Lesley Cameron
Cover and interior design by April Tran
Photography by Callum Kyllonen

CATALOGUING INFORMATION AVAILABLE FROM LIBRARY AND ARCHIVES CANADA
ISBN 9781771514354 (hardcover)
ISBN 9781771514385 (electronic)

TouchWood Editions acknowledges that the land on which we live and work is within the traditional territories of the Lkwungen (Esquimalt and Songhees), Malahat, Pacheedaht, Scia'new, T'Sou-ke, and W̱SÁNEĆ (Pauquachin, Tsartlip, Tsawout, and Tseycum) peoples.

We acknowledge the financial support of the Government of Canada through the Canada Book Fund, and the province of British Columbia through the Book Publishing Tax Credit.

This book was produced using FSC®-certified, acid-free papers, processed chlorine free, and printed with soya-based inks.

Printed in China

28 27 26 25 24 1 2 3 4 5